Oil Tankers and Speedboats

'The skill of writing is to create a context
in which other people can think.'
— Edwin Schlossberg

MENNO LANTING

Oil Tankers and Speedboats

AGILITY AT WORK IN THE 21ST CENTURY

Business Contact Publishers
Amsterdam/Antwerp

© 2015 Menno Lanting
Business Contact Publishers
Original title *Olietankers en speedboten*
Translation by Martha Wagteveld-Osborn
Cover design Bart van den Tooren
Interior design Zeno
Author photo Arno Massee

ISBN 978 90 470 0909 2

www.businesscontact.nl

Table of contents

Foreword 7
Introduction 11

   1   Stormy weather 21
   2   Charting a new course 39
   3   From oil tanker to speedboat 59
   4   From speedboat to oil tanker 79
   5   A fleet of speedboats 99
   6   Seven principles for agility in work, learning and business 119
   7   Getting the best hands on deck 149
   8   The captain as the hidden force 165

Epilogue 187
Notes 191

Foreword

It was just over a year ago that I sat down to compare and contrast my ideas on work and business in our tumultuous times against the thoughts of people I am inspired by: founders and employees of cool start-ups, CEOs of well-established businesses and self-employed professionals who travel the world as free agents. I was transported the world over by this plan of mine, from the Dutch lowlands to the sophisticated and metropolitan Barcelona, Beijing, Dubai, Geneva, Hong Kong, London, New York, San Francisco and Washington.

All in all, I spoke with nearly one hundred people. With their help, I was able to structure my own ideas, and they kept providing me with new insights. This book will bring you quotes from these conversations. For instance, these words uttered by John Sculley, former president of PepsiCo and former CEO of Apple: *"It is virtually impossible to explain to anyone under thirty how complicated it was, doing business in the pre-digital age. Nowadays, leadership has an increased openness and is more equally-footed in its structure. Organizations that have grasped this tend to have no walls, nor do their staff have fixed desks or offices. I no longer have an office myself; my laptop case is my office. I can work at conferences, in hotels, cafés and airports. The entire business world has changed completely."*

In San Francisco, I met with Stephen Roberts, the former CTO of US retailer Best Buy. Upon mentioning the working title for this book, *Digital leadership*, he urged me, from his heart: *"Please do not call your book that, it is complete and utter non-*

sense. If you do, you turn the digital transformation into something separate, something 'on the side'. We will then continue to regard it as such, and people will not view it as the very essence of their skill set, which it in fact is. Speed is key, as is the ability to change, to experiment, to fail and to learn. In a word, that is the core of our work and business in this century."

Roberts is no lone wolf in this respect. Back in 1971, Daniel Callahan, philosopher of biomedical ethics, wrote presciently: *"We have to do away with a false and misleading dualism, one which abstracts man on the one hand and technology on the other, as if the two were quite separate kinds of realities... Man is by nature a technological animal; to be human is to be technological. We should recognize that when we speak of technology, this is another way of speaking about man himself in one of his manifestations."*

Stephen Roberts was spot on. Digital leadership is not what matters; what you do or fail to do with digital tools, as a leader, manager, entrepreneur or professional, is not what matters. What does matter is whether you are able to adjust in order to continue contributing to your work; if you are able to take charge of the many changes in your surroundings, and the adjustments you are then required to make. To me, the word 'leadership' is not connected to the position you have within an organization. It is all about showing initiative, and deciding on a direction for your own life and work in a world in flux.

The term I use for those professionals and organizations who succeed at this is 'speedboats', whereas I refer to organizations that cling to their former course of action as 'oil tankers'. A wonderful metaphor, though I am quick to admit that any kind of sharply defined juxtaposition in the title will inevitably conjure up images, and provoke a strong reaction. After all, an oil tanker is slow, and being slow often means you tend to lag behind, and end up being decidedly uncool, to boot. On the other hand, a speedboat brings to mind all kinds of pictures of speed, agility and dynamic movement. To be sure, in practice, things are not so black-and-white. Over the past few months, I have received messages from several people to tell me that, in fact, oil tankers are agile too, particularly if I were to account for their huge size, but that speedboats are actually quite a nuisance to fishing boats. This kind of thing really does make an author's day. Then I received several pleas to not use oil tankers or speedboats in the title, and to opt for sailing boats instead. Were they not agile and environmentally friendly, too? Just imagine, the publisher and I had at one time contemplated a book cover with an elephant and a mouse, or with a giant and Tom Thumb. In the end then, I settled on Oil Tankers and Speedboats!

Regardless of whether you go for oil tankers, giants, sailing boats or speedboats, 'adaptability' is the main theme for this book: being able to transcend what you were educated for, or the career path you may have taken, the business models you had faith in, how relevant you deemed your organization, and how you thought it would remain that way for decades to come, all these things, you need to transcend and by doing so, accept that we are truly making the transition from the industrial age to the networking era.

How to use this book

I will not be handing you a manual on how to read this book. Just start at the beginning, or the end, or just leaf through the pages randomly. After all, it is up to you. If you are stuck for time, may I suggest you at least read Chapter 6? This is basically a summary of sorts of the whole book.

Researching and writing this book has been an immensely enjoyable journey for me. I hope I can share this with you, the reader. Apart from the conversations I had, I found inspiration in numerous various online and offline media, reports and articles alike. I have done my utmost, going to great lengths, to source the original citations and include them in my endnotes. However, if by chance I have overlooked anything, do let me know. Besides, I am very keen to know what effect this book has on you. Please send me any questions, comments to @mlanting or mennolanting@gmail.com.

A big thank you for your time and enjoy the read!

Menno Lanting

Introduction

In the past few years, the City of Philadelphia has managed to downsize its team of garbage collectors from 33 employees to 17. How did they pull that off? Did its citizens put out less trash? Did people start to illegally burn their waste in the backyard? Far from it. In 2009, the BigBelly Solar Company installed 'intelligent trash compaction units' equipped with software that enabled the company to see which bin needed to be emptied when. By using this information, it was possible to reduce the number of times that waste was collected from seventeen times a week to just three.[1]

The city of Barcelona uses similar technology and is hoping to find clever solutions in a variety of other fields too. Sensors are already being installed all over the conurbation to measure traffic intensity and inform drivers of their expected travel time. Forty percent of the municipal parks have automatic sprinklers and 50,000 households – mainly the elderly and less mobile – have access to an online helpdesk. In order to facilitate these developments, the city council has provided a large proportion of the data collected by the city to its citizens and businesses. They are then invited to think up new technological solutions.[2] Barcelona has the ambition to save 3 billion euros over the next decade, mainly on salaries.[3]

Barcelona and Philadelphia have proven to be examples for other cities too. The Finnish capital Helsinki is using sensors and GPS to allow snow trucks to drive the most efficient route possible. *"Most importantly, these services are aimed at making life easier for citizens. A subsequent benefit for us is that it helps us reduce physical labor,"* says Kari Miskala, head of the ICT Development Team.[4]

Obsolete

There are more examples of similar kinds of digitization: back in 2011, McDonalds announced its resolve to replace part of the workforce with touch screens.[5] Personal assistants will become partly or completely obsolete if you can use your tablet or smartphone to easily manage your calendar yourself. Should you have any difficulty in doing so, there are always digital assistants, like Google Now or Siri.[6, 7] If you prefer some degree of human contact, there are thousands of 'virtual' English speaking assistants to wait on you, in countries like India, Kenya and Tanzania, at a fraction of the cost of a personal assistant. Jeff Bezos, founder of e-commerce company Amazon, fired all his reviewers when he discovered software was far better at doing the job, and that automatically-generated reviews led to higher sales besides.[8] Amazon is by no means a loner in this: in time, highly-sophisticated algorithms are expected to take over 140 million full time jobs of knowledge workers.[9]

What are the implications of such change for motoring clubs – the Dutch ANWB is as good an example as any – when in the foreseeable future our cars will be able to give advance warning of a potential defect, long before it happens, so that we can just drive into the workshop long before we end up with a breakdown at the roadside? What would we then need our traditional subscription to their roadside assistance?[10] How many ANWB employees – some 5,000 in all, including more than 800 patrol staff – will become surplus to requirements?

What about taxi drivers? Pioneer Uber is not only shaking up the business model of the taxi industry, but may well undermine the very raison d'être of the profession. What if it were to start using self-driving cars in the future?[11, 12]

The digital era

New developments occurring in quick succession surely are a sign of the times. Google's Chief Economist Hal Varian labels this 'combinatorial innovation'. He states there have been times like these throughout the course of history, each with their own characteristics. The age of industry saw the mechanization of production and parts becoming interchangeable for the first time ever; easily replaceable too. In the IT/internet era computers took over calculations and we all became interconnected through our PCs.

Now we have come to the digital era, where we are able to develop new products and services courtesy of mobile technology. Digital ingredients – bits and bytes – cost next to nothing, are in infinite supply and enable a myriad of product/market combinations. Virtually everyone can access these bits and bytes, and they are invariably easy to copy and distribute.

Organizations are noticeably being affected by this digital revolution. Technological innovation in the 21st century is no longer the special reserve of larger organizations, due to almost ubiquitous access to these digital building blocks. The market for innovation is open to small and mid-sized businesses, and even to individuals. Large and often cumbersome organizations now have to deal with strong competition from start-ups.

Oil tankers and speedboats

Prior to the age of internet, innovation had a relative predictability. It was accomplished by the R&D department within the organization, according to a set pattern.[13] Nowadays people – be they individuals or their networks – adopt new technology faster than organizations can keep up with them. This is giving birth to new and agile businesses, which like speedboats are able to use any angle to zip past the large established organizations-or the oil tankers.

A list of the fifty most innovative companies worldwide has very few multinationals on it.[14] In fact, the bulk of them are small, though their innovative product does have a global impact. Dropbox, for instance, has a very small team that provides cloud services. Just picture GitHub, with its platform where programmers can work on projects together, or Netflix, head-butting established media with streaming video. The list is endless.

A focus on innovation does pay off, that much is crystal clear. On the stock market, innovative companies are outperforming their less innovative industry counterparts by up to 200 percent.[15] Besides, of all the companies on the Fortune 500 in the year 2000, over 40 percent no longer exist.[16]

WhatsApp, Snapchat and the like have used their chat services to bring the huge telecom companies tumbling down. There are masses of stories about 'traditional businesses' being struck down by new business models. A Dutch case in point: the Free Record Shop chain went belly up through a fierce digital storm of illegal downloads and alternative suppliers like iTunes, Spotify and Google Music.[17] Their classical overheads for retail shops and staff were just too expensive for them to compete with online alternatives. At their demise, their turnover was still an impressive 300 million euros, but their profits were only a scant 1.5 million euros; a mere 7 euro cents per customer. No way could that cover their overhead. *"The business failed to respond quickly enough to changes in the marketplace,"* observed one of the receivers. *"They could clearly see it happening, but their responses were just inadequate."*[18]

Similarly, bookshop chains are having to close down or otherwise morph into speedboats in order to serve their customers properly, moving away from the anonymity of the huge oil tanker.[19] Travel agents are increasingly irrelevant, and the same is true for any sort of intermediary, be it advisory bodies, lawyers or training agencies. The consultancy business has plummeted by some 20 percent since 2008.[20] The internet has given customers quicker and easier access to new tools, concepts and models.[21]

The annual CEO Survey conducted by IBM shows CEOs rightly citing technology as the key external influence on their organizations.[22] Consumers uniting online and rapidly taking their share of the power formerly belonging to the oil tankers are but one example. Then there are the start-ups that serve consumers with ICT tools, faster and better than before, often by providing another added value or even by meeting a different need entirely. All this may well sound self-evident, but until quite recently the impact of digital technology was not taken into account seriously in most board rooms. Consequently, employees were not given an adequate understanding of how this technology would set the world in rapid turmoil, nor of how it would affect the organization and their individual jobs.

A whole new set of rules

The world is changing: old laws and models are proving to be useless, new ones are being devised on the go. On the one hand, the world seems to be getting smaller through all the digital communication, even though all these connections also make life more complicated. The mere demise of a few companies is just the tip of the iceberg; in actual fact one era is being ushered out, as the new one comes in and takes center stage. We are gradually moving from the age of industry into the digital era, and ultimately this will affect every one of us. This inbound dynamic necessitates a new way of structuring organizations: less overhead, a real minimum of unnecessary hierarchy, more autonomy for professionals and consequently fewer managers.

Responsiveness

A staggering 87% of employees worldwide are not engaged at work. The world has a crisis of engagement, having serious and potentially long-lasting repercussions for the global economy.[23]

I witnessed an interesting example of this when I was visiting Dubai, in the United Arab Emirates. *"As policy makers we are constantly looking ahead. The world is changing so rapidly, that we cannot afford even the briefest lapse in attention. We need to keep adapting,"* says Mohammad Al Hawi, Head of Innovation in the Executive Office of the President. Until the 1960s, the Arab states, which were still separate, reaped most of their earnings from the sales of dates and pearls. Then they struck oil.

An unparalleled wealth was tapped into. As it soon became clear that the oil supplies were to run out after roughly a century, a substantial chunk of the money earned in the oil industry was used to build an impressive infrastructure and a highly professional finance and tourism industry. Today oil makes up a mere 5 percent of total revenues. *"In spite of our success, we are already working hard on our next move,"* Al Hawi continues while I am being served with tea and dates. The next move will be an open-armed embrace of the technological and digital revolution: *"In a few years, we would like to have a business atmosphere conducive to building companies like Facebook, Samsung, Google and Spotify ourselves. Currently we are investing billions to upgrade our level of education, concerning new digital technology, thus drawing creative talent the world over to us, and realizing a climate of experiment."*

One could say that things happen more quickly in an authoritarian state, but the ambition in itself is certainly one to inspire. A similar attitude could well help us take giant steps in the West, too. There does not seem to be any high level awareness of the need for change, neither in politics nor in business.

Fewer jobs

Anytime countries and regions are in trouble, businesses fold, and that means job losses. The same can be said for jobs disappearing when technology replaces people. Research has made clear that approximately half the current jobs in the United States are expected to disappear in the near future, as a result of digitization and ongoing automation.[24] Whether or not Europe and the Netherlands will be similarly affected, still remains to be seen.

Technology has now brought us to the eve of an era in which robots will be used for any number of tasks, and not just for routine, heavy or filthy factory labor.[25] According to Neil Jacobstein, Co-chair of the Robotics Faculty at Singularity University in the Silicon Valley, robots will relieve us of a lot of work: standard production work, to be sure, but also routine knowledge work such as checking tax returns. Physicians will have digital assistants, who are able to process far larger chunks of information than the human counterpart.[26]

New opportunities

However, jobs and business models are not simply disappearing into thin air, as the digital revolution is providing opportunities of its own. Plenty of them, in fact. It remains to be seen whether they will create sufficient added value to give credence to the existing structures. To put it differently, it is quite possible that we will, generally speaking, need fewer people, buildings, company cars, and so on, to reach the same or greater added value than before. At the same time, the question arises as to whether everyone will be able to seamlessly exchange one job or one business model for another. Jaron Lanier is correct in pointing out that the current middle class is very much at risk of ending up in serious trouble, if we do nothing and decide not to go with the flow.[27]

These are relevant developments for all of us, executives and employees alike. No longer are business models set in stone, nor is social relevance or decades of working for the same company. Oil tankers that have been charting the same steady course for years, and which deem it less than desirable and possibly even dangerous to change course, need to give the wheel a hefty tug. Now, the course must be altered constantly, and the very structure of organizations is characterized by change. We need to adapt to a new reality, in which our lives and work are deeply involved with technology.

> **"We do not 'simply' experience another alteration of the business cycles, rather a restructuring of our economic order."**
> – IAN DAVIS, MCKINSEY[28]

Intuitive leadership

This book is intended to be read by managers, professionals and business people, who are curious as to what their roles will be in the future: people who are keen to discover what their added value will be in a more loosely-structured organization, where employees are increasingly well-equipped to organize their own work. This may sound like a paradox but such organizations certainly do need unison and direction. In other words, strong leadership. To be sure, it will have different contours than those we are accustomed to; frequently leadership will be shared, and temporary at that. This digital era, in which we reach an unsurpassed level of connecting with each other on shared topics, has in fact acquired the best ever conditions for leadership with the greatest common ground. Never before have there been so many leaders, despite not regarding themselves as such, who have started a movement of some kind. Leadership has many different faces. A person who leaves an organization and takes a gang of people with him is just as much a leader of that company as the CEO is. Leadership is a prerequisite for the steps we collectively need to take.

Why is it so hard to transition from the age of industry to the digital era? As I was writing this book, I have constantly kept this question in mind. The answer is probably that we have been taught to listen to our rational mind, instead of our intuition. Within organizations, our measure is often taken based on where we went to school or university, how many hours a week we work, what our boss thinks about a certain topic, whether or not we will have finished the quarterly report on time, our attendance at all meetings, etcetera.

The potential of the mind is infinite, and yet rather prone to limiting itself at the same time— or so neuroscience has taught us. In general, and particularly in the workplace, we are inclined to focus on our mind over anything else. We have learnt to ignore our instinct and to listen to 'the boss'.

Being influenced by their experiences of all the possibilities of the internet, people are rapidly letting go of the habit of listening to their boss. Everywhere they look, alternatives are readily available. It is omnipresent in politics, in media and most importantly in the relationship between consumers and businesses, and citizens and government. More than ever before, people will chart their own course, without taking too much notice of now obsolete structures, or of debilitating hierarchies. Managers, professionals and business people quickly need to find a way to get swept up in this movement.

1. Stormy weather

Clouded by jetlag, I arrive at San Francisco airport. Without thinking properly, I emerge stumbling from the endless queue at customs into a battered old taxi. My thoughts are of a hot meal and then, bed. Mustering the energy to say a friendly hello to the driver is almost more than I can manage. He ignores me. I wonder about his hearing and repeat my cordial greeting, louder now. No response. In the meantime, the taxi has moved away from the airport and turned onto the highway. Interesting really, as I have yet to express where I would like to go. My jetlag catches up with me and, mildly annoyed, I ask where on earth we are heading. I can barely make out his curt answer: "*To the downtown hotels, of course.*" He apparently thinks that is where all tourists and business men go. He takes quite some convincing before he realizes I am in fact headed for a suburb, where I am renting an apartment. He is adamant in his disagreement. He almost growls at me as he asks me why on earth I am staying there, before making a terrifying U-turn in the middle of the highway – thank heavens there is no hard shoulder – to take the taxi in the right direction. Or has he really? I cannot help noticing on Google Maps, where I am tracking our journey, that he is taking a wild detour. When we finally reach the neighborhood, the driver actually needs to borrow my iPhone to use the same Google Maps to drop me at the end of the street. "You can walk the rest." Dumbfounded by jetlag, I get out of the cab, only to find him lowering his creaky window and demanding a tip.

This experience cured me from ever using 'normal' taxis again. Even without this excessive incident, I am very rarely impressed by the quality provided by taxis and their drivers. Ever since my visit to San Francisco, I have used the Uber-app to book a cab. GPS shows me a little map with the taxis in my vicinity. In order to avoid another run-in with a driver who lacks people skills, I only pick taxis with a four or five-star rating (each passenger is able to leave a review after a ride). I then receive an invoice – which I pay with a previously registered credit card – and I can check the route chosen by the driver on a little map, to see if it is indeed the quickest. Oh, and by the way, Uber only uses black town cars. This is very helpful, as it means you often spot your ride en route, helped too by GPS on the map. The driver greets you on a first-name basis, to ensure you do not hop into the wrong car by mistake.

It is not just the traditional taxi trade in San Francisco, or any other city I visit for that matter, that I no longer do business with – hotels too are not taking as much of my cash as before either. The apartment where the cab driver from hell finally deposited me was rented through Airbnb, the online marketplace where people rent out their room, apartment or house directly. A clearly-presented website with a helpful map and plenty of search options, it displays accommodation at a far more attractive price-to-quality ratio than most hotels. An added bonus is the pleasure of meeting actual locals.

"Uber is a 3.5 billion lesson in building a world how it ought to be, instead of optimizing the world as it is."
– AARON LEVIE, CO-FOUNDER AND CEO OF BOX

Not only is Airbnb an innovative platform, it has been thought through properly, providing people with an indispensable sense of trust. Renting out your home to someone you have never met is quite daunting, after all, and the same is true for staying with a complete stranger. An effective solution: guests write reviews of their stay and hosts write one of their own, about the guests. Deceptively simple, but the second review makes me want to be a better guest; I am gratified by leaving a place behind in such a way that the owner will give me a good review.

In transit

The taxi and hospitality industry are by no means alone in their added value being scrutinized; organizations in all kinds of industries are feeling the pressure. Current changes, often technological, are proving hard for organizations to keep up with. Newcomers like Airbnb and Uber spot opportunities and grab them. Increasing speed of innovation, and adapting strategy and thinking outside the box, these are prerequisites for organizations now. Being aware of emerging patterns and the bigger picture, correctly assessing new platforms, or better yet, setting them up for yourself. The most significant change is that consumers are longing for a whole new user experience, one more personal and faster too.

It is by no means a seamless transition. New entrants like Airbnb and Uber need to be prepared for fierce resistance from established businesses.[1] They often stretch the limits of current legislation, which tends to develop at a rather slower rate than the world of change.[2] Most organizations and their leaders, however, have begun to realize that business and organizing have been forever changed.

Disruptive market innovations have always been around, but there has been a seismic shift of late. In the past there was a clearly visible pattern: new parties entered the market, most likely with a cheaper alternative and gradually acquired their share of the market.[3] A large organization had no less of a guarantee of succeeding, though the oil tanker would have enough time to change its course. This is down to the gradual nature of market growth on the part of the competition. Today there are more 'Big Bang innovations' than ever, a term coined by Larry Downes and Paul F. Nunes in *Big Bang Disruption*. Often these take place in the wake of a quick succession of cheap experiments. The internet is generally the distribution channel of choice, reaching large numbers of consumers rapidly and creating expeditious growth.

New innovation curve

Our high level of connectedness online enables us to discover new products and services in the blink of an eye. Boredom is always lurking while we yearn for something new, immediately. The waiting game is a bad idea for anyone in business, as is waiting to see what the competition is up to and taking your cues accordingly. You will invariably turn up late at the proverbial party. You really need to make innovation an investment priority.

> **"Even if you are on the right track, if you are waiting around you will inevitably be crushed to bits."**
> – ACTOR WILL ROGERS

Innovation of procedures or of products, those are your options.[4] The first applies to rejuvenating your business and organizational models; the latter is about radically new products or services. They often involve conquering a completely new market. This in turn calls for an entrepreneurial spirit all too often lacking in large organizations. Broadly speaking, they are particularly focused on providing efficient service to an existing market, utilizing products and services that are just ever so slightly tweaked, over and over. New businesses tend to show more of the required pioneering and risk-taking attitude.[5]

Run aground

Once in a while, a large organization will succeed in overtaking the *disruptor* and conquer the new market after all.[6] This is, however, a strategy which is hard to plan and fraught with risks. If the oil tanker proves to have taken the wrong course and subsequently runs aground, this will often be irreversible. This is exactly what happened to Nokia.[7] Stephen Elop – then CEO of Nokia – wrote an email to all the Nokia staff in 2011: *"We poured gasoline on our own burning platform. I believe we have lacked accountability and leadership to align and direct the company through these disruptive times. We had a series of misses. We haven't been delivering innovation fast enough. We're not collaborating internally. Nokia, our platform is burning."*[8] Elop was well aware of the forces Nokia was battling. In that same memo he said: *"Chinese*

OEMs are cranking out a device much faster than, as one Nokia employee said only partially in jest, 'the time that it takes us to polish a PowerPoint presentation.' They are fast, they are cheap, and they are challenging us." His words came true within no time at all. The Chinese company Xiaomi (had you ever heard of them then?) launched a new phone in 2013 and sold 100,000 units within 86 seconds.[9] (Elop then 'moved along' to Microsoft, as part of the takeover.)

Another giant, Shell, is by no means immune to these developments. *"The world is changing at an increasing pace, and disruptive innovations are changing how we work, live, are organized and communicate,"* according to Thijs Jurgens, their Vice President of Innovation. *"Technology is increasingly complex. Integrating technology is an art in itself. This may well surpass the capabilities of any organization, even one of our magnitude."*[10]

The ability to move with a changing market is especially challenging for large companies. Disruptive innovations tend to develop in niche markets, often because end users are thinking up their own solutions for urgent problems.[11] Those users are often ahead of the bunch, and hardly expecting a new product or service to work without a glitch.[12] Disruptive innovation often takes established businesses by surprise, as it appears from an unexpected angle. For instance, navigation company TomTom was completely taken off guard by all manner of free navigation apps, which succeeded in significantly disrupting the business model.[13]

Henk Volberda, business economist and Professor of Strategic Management and Entrepreneurial Policy at the Erasmus University Rotterdam, believes that – in spite of businesses toppling over left, right and center – 11 percent of Dutch businesses do nothing whatsoever to innovate their business model, and another 21 percent make only a slight effort. A sizeable chunk, 29 percent, does actually make 'some attempts' at innovation. Volberda thinks it is precisely this group, which is 'still on the fence' so to speak, who could do with a nudge of encouragement to stimulate the competitiveness of the Dutch economy.

Martec's Law

As these developments take on a more definite shape, we are now stumbling into real obstacles. Blogger and entrepreneur Scott Brinker refers to this as 'Martec's Law'.[14] This refers to how technological possibilities tend to grow at an exponential rate, whereas organizations are inclined to develop at a more leisurely pace. Brinker has based the first part of this law on two other laws, or codes, of technology: 1) Moore's Law, which makes clear that computer arithmetic doubles its speed roughly every two years, while its cost declines by only half in the same time period; and 2) Metcalfe's Law, describing how the value of network connections increases, proportionate to the size of the network. An organization's capacity for change, however, remains more restrained. Structures set in stone, natural resistance and vested interests all stand in the way of fast adaptation. And change fatigue, paired with cynicism are all making sure that, in fact, the willingness to change is actually declining.

Mark Frissora, former CEO of car rental firm Hertz, has this to say: *"Technology is constantly challenging traditional business models, and it happens faster and faster in ways that can be difficult to see. When a new technology emerges, companies need to decide almost immediately whether to adopt it—or they could risk being destroyed by it."*[15]

In a leaked internal report, eminent newspaper *The New York Times* admits to its failure: *"We noticed our readers moving en masse to social media, while we were still doing a redesign of our homepage."*[16] And really, this is just the beginning, of all the changes digital technology will produce. Cisco CEO John Chambers remarks: *"The most significant transition we shall experience is when we start to connect everything – and I do mean everything – in a virtual sense. This will impact countries' productivity. Alter business models and we alter our day-to-day lives. Its impact (of connectivity) on our society will be 5 to 10 times greater than internet has had."*[7]

The right culture

As an organization, Google tries to fly in the face of almost every convention and urges their employees, partners and suppliers to adopt a different view of reality. In so doing, they may well face resistance, but they are able to produce new perspectives that disrupt entire industries. Just picture the self-driving car, or the development of wearable technology, or making the internet freely available to all, and various payment option initiatives.[18] All these things spring from a culture where professionals are encouraged to excel and where ideas 'flow' freely.[19]

> **"Invention is made up of seeing what everyone else has seen, and then thinking of something no one has previously come up with."**
> – ALBERT SZENT-GYÖRGI, HUNGARIAN PHYSICIAN AND NOBEL PRIZE WINNER

Canadian telecom company Telus is another example, of an organization 'genetically' predisposed to innovation and new ideas. Dan Pontefract, Chief Envisioner, states in an interview: *"At the end of the day your culture is going to speak to how well you are going to do in a competitive environment, and if you have a culture of people that are somewhere between apathetic and unenthused, then are you really going to be an innovative organization? Are you really going to be best in class, or the place where everyone's dropping off their résumé?"*[20] Apple, too, has an innate understanding of the importance of culture. Steve Jobs once said, *"Innovation has nothing to do with how many R&D dollars you have. When Apple came up with the Mac, IBM was spending at least 100 times more on R&D. It's not about money. It's about the people you have, how you're led, and how much you get it."*[21]

Better the listener than the transmitter

Apart from the right culture, a deeper understanding of what consumers want will become increasingly important to businesses. The evolution of the 'shared economy' should prove useful here: already, various start-ups use the internet as a means to match individual supply and demand. This has sparked a transition from 'possession' to 'access'. Airbnb and Uber, mentioned previously, are prime examples, though car-sharing services like SnappCar and Zipcar are another two. Large established market players idly stood by and watched, until the emerging pattern became clear to them. BMW jumped on the bandwagon and now provides consumers with a method to share BMWs, through DriveNow. The company has ambitiously set itself a target of having 1 million customers by 2020, in Germany alone.[22]

> **"First of all, let us bring added value to consumers. We can figure out how it will make us money, later on."**
> – ASTRO TELLER, CAPTAIN OF MOONSHOTS GOOGLE X

Mark Frissora, too, noticed Hertz being overtaken by the far smaller company Zipcar: *"This new way of renting cars would have been easy to ignore; Zipcar was a small player, and only in big cities. But we knew the technology itself—and related developments such as software apps like Uber—would be transformational, and we knew these ideas could move up the value chain and really disrupt business models. So we embraced them, because it's better to use a new technology to transform your own business than to watch your competitors beat you to it."*[23]

Quite often, the consumer has harnessed their massive power of information, to become the proactive and leading party, relating to business and government alike, be it in the realm of travel, banking and insurance, going out or shopping.[24] Brian Solis, in *What's the Future of Business,* continues this train of thought. He argues that creating experiences beyond the expectations of consumers is what matters now, as is tying into their need for communicating, and developing and setting themselves apart from others. Not many organizations have set out to create this kind of 'wow-experience' yet, but rather opt for besieging us with unwanted marketing efforts. As a result, they often lose precious time and money in responding to (frequently negative) experiences of consumers. All this they bring upon themselves, instead of proactively remarking on these very experiences, or developing them and providing them at the appropriate time and place, in such a fashion that they may be shared on social networks.

Let users participate in development

Another perceptible trend is how products and services are becoming a more significant part of our identities. John Sculley said: *"When I was hired at Apple in 1983, Steve Jobs told me that the computer would become a personal item, not a piece of technology, but an extension of your identity, a magnificently designed object, that would help you to live a better and more creative life. From that very moment, Apple became diametrically different to the PC."* An organization is then required to choose a completely altered approach, and not onlyas regards product and service development. Virtually everything an organization does needs to happen in the market; it should be tested there and adjusted too. In fact, businesses ought to ensure the market is part of their organization. Steve Jobs once remarked: *"You need to set out from the consumer experience and work back to technology from there, not the other way around."*[25] It is so self-evident: I never cease to be amazed how businesses fail to collaborate with the people they aim to serve.

At a large conference in London, when I spoke with Monika Fahlbusch, former Senior Vice President for Global Employee Success and Chief Culture Officer at Salesforce.com – incidentally one of the fastest growing companies in the world – she told me: *"If you want to change businesses, you ought to examine how the way people communicate has changed. The world has become 'social', networks of consumers. Citizens and employees have become immensely powerful. I pick up on this whenever I look at our employees, who are 34 years old on average. They are highly connected to each other, similar to the way my children in their twenties were connected to their favorite brands. It is impossible to ignore this. You should meet your customers and staff at the place where they already are. Increasingly, their networks are the platforms where we are able to develop new products and services. We*

must listen to them extremely carefully, and equally embrace that
social world, as they do, and subsequently become part of it. This is
the only way to genuinely understand the new world, and to remain
relevant in it, be it as a business, professional or leader."

The beauty of technology is how it provides the means for
detailed listening to consumers or citizens thus enabling the dis-
covery of what is important to them. Former Google Chief Technology Officer, Michele R. Weslander-Quaid, tells me about the
launch of social network Google+ in a beta version. A team of
developers was on standby to provide instant solutions for any
mistakes or omissions that users might share online. At the time
of its launch, Google+ was only approximately 80 percent finished, the rest was completed through interacting with users.

What these examples make clear is the central place leaders
need to offer their customers. I would love to see leaders have
as profound an understanding of their consumers' lives as they
do of their company's income and expenditure account. All too
often, it would be an immense help to get rid of the marketing
department, and give the responsibility for marketing to actual
product managers, enforcing a need for them to walk a mile in
the shoes belonging to their customers.

Resistance

It is more the lack of willingness to innovate, rather than the ability to do so, that is the real problem for traditional market leaders. Amazon CEO, Jeff Bezos, has remained supremely focused
on the internal resistance to change throughout the prolific
growth of his company. In his experience, even within the most
innovative and strongest companies people are inclined to resist
change and unorthodox experiments. In order to openly discuss
this natural tendency, Bezos asked each of the directors he spoke
to for a personal example of resisting a new development. He
simply meant to open up the discussion of that very resistance
and how to deal with it.[26]

Bezos' vision is backed up by a wide range of research. To
name one, Pierre Azoulay was able to show that when researchers are given much leeway to research over a length of time,

there is a noticeable increase of innovation occurring. It is particularly crucial that researchers are provoked to take risks, and not let themselves be discouraged by failures. *"If you wish to urge people to explore unproven avenues, then you need to reward for long-term success, give great freedom to experiment and tolerate early failures,"* Azoulay explains.[27]

Many times this calls for adjusting internal politics within an organization, as this is often the cause of risk-adverse behavior. Sometimes outside intervention is needed. Innovation after all never happens without plenty of failures, and it is precisely that which is penalized by internal politics. Of course, the frontrunners need to be associated with those politics; however, I have seldom seen systems undergo changes that were wholly operated from outside the organization.

> **"Any company that is not challenging the status quo will not survive."**
> – GAVIN PATTERSON, CEO BT

Success and failure: a fine line

John Sculley is a person familiar with the challenges of large companies trying to adapt to their altered surroundings, and he is now a mentor and investor for several 'serial entrepreneurs'. The sparkling septuagenarian and I meet each other at San Francisco airport, where he is in transit on one of his many trips. Our encounter is in the arrivals terminal. In the midst of passing hordes of tourists and business people, he imparts his outlook on leadership and the required development of organizations: *"For decades, I have focused on what you might call 'transformative business', i.e. those industries that are highly susceptible to change, and that dance the fine line between success and failure. I too have noticed that the most interesting and promising innovations occur on the very cusp; where things start to get exciting."* Markets have become more transparent, according to Sculley, and consequently more competitive, though there is now also more room to collaborate. *"In the 1980s, before any of us had internet, email or smartphones, all the knowledge was locked inside organizations and in the brains of people who derived power from it. We could not speak to other people from the industry, without a lawyer being present. And should* you happen to work for Pepsi, and accidentally be in the same place as someone from Coca-Cola, you simply had to leave."

Sculley is keen to emphasize how the current speed of external development influences organizations: "It is not long ago that you would have needed a minimum of ten to fifteen million dollars, to make even the tiniest possible impact, as a newcomer. Now, the cost of entering into any given market is lower than ever, due to all that has happened in ICT. A small team of programmers, paired with a good idea and a server, and you can be on your way. In the United States, at least, it is possible to set up a business within 24 hours, while most businesses are still structured according to a radically different time frame. In the 1980s it took Apple seven years to change the IOS. Just imagine, seven years! Today, it could not be more different. No one ventures into time-consuming software development; it no longer works. This is all because of the emergence of apps. They are made quickly and, if they turn out not to work, they are just as quickly replaced by new ones. Speed is key, as are short lines, frequent tries, and quickly dropping something if it does not work."

Sculley believes the beauty of this all to be that technology is no longer limiting, in other words, it can now be of enormous help to keep the relevant procedures up to speed. "As I mentioned before, the developments involving cloud, mobile and virtualization, are all responsible for the possibility of starting out with something small and it still making a huge splash." The former Apple executive is adamant that timing is everything. He refers to Apple's first tablet, Newton, which proved to be a miserable failure:[29] "We made it at least fifteen to twenty years early."

Mistakes

We keep on making the mistake of presuming to know which direction technology will take, when in fact it ends up charting an entirely different course. Kevin Kelly, founder of *Wired* and author of several books, describes how wrong we were in our interpretation of the future of the internet,[30] in *What Technology Wants*. We thought it would be a kind of television 2.0, where we would develop several bespoke 'channels', each providing information on a specific field of interest. Instead it most frequently proved to be a means for people to share their own content.

And we have seen nothing yet, compared to what is in store for us, as Kelly says: *"But the next twenty years are going to make these past twenty years just pale. We're just at the beginning of the beginning of all these kind of changes. There's a sense that all the big things have happened, but relatively speaking, nothing big has happened yet."*

According to Kelly, we need years of intensive training – similar to learning how to read and write – to learn to handle new media: *"While there's Internet speed of life, which is going very fast, we are biological beings and there's generations of investment infrastructure that will take a long time to pay off* [...] *it'll take us another generation before we actually understand what the Web is."*

> **"You don't understand anything, until you learn it in more than one way."**
> – MARVIN MINSKY, PROFESSOR OF MEDIA ARTS AND SCIENCES AT MIT MEDIA LAB AND MIT AI LAB

Technology: part of the organization's DNA

Even though it is unclear which technology will prove to be relevant, businesses face the crucial decision of stepping onto the playing field now, particularly for those developments that have begun to take shape, but have not yet been translated into actual market demands. On becoming CEO at Microsoft, Sadya Nadella admitted that he regarded a continued ability to pick up speed as key for the organization, and his own personal goal to boot: *"Microsoft faces a huge opportunity for the taking, but to actually grab it, we must move faster, focus more and continue to transform. To my mind, making sure our customers have access to our product innovations faster is a large part of my job."*[31]

Rajiv Pant, Chief Technology Officer of *The New York Times*, is specific in his mention of technology as one of the most important instruments to reach the required speed. He knows what he is on about; after all, the news industry has been particularly affected by all the changes. The innovation report, already referred to, drives home this point powerfully: *"Our daily report is deep, broad, smart and engaging — and we've got a huge lead over the competition. At the same time, we are falling behind in a second critical area: the art and science of getting our journalism to readers. We have always cared about the reach and impact of our work, but we haven't done enough to crack that code in the digital era."*[32]

I discuss this with Pant in New York. He believes it is vital for virtually any organization to afford technology a central and strategic role: *"Technology has made a real shift away from the side-lines. In the past I worked for companies where the top IT position was the data processing manager. They did not even have a Director of Technology."* Since then *The New York Times* (and probably every other organization too) has masses of people in a technological role, be it at times indirectly. People who work on lay-out, who produce visuals based on data; marketing professionals who roll out online campaigns; experts on internal communication experimenting with Yammer; and so on. According to Pant, this turns almost everyone into a 'techie', and makes it essential for staff to use the same tools of technology for their clients. This is particularly true for leaders, even if they are not of a generation that was raised with these tools: *"An organization needs to adequately reflect the society his clients belong to. [...] The challenges faced by the average organization are so immense, that diversity in backgrounds, experiences and ideas is vital, more than it ever was."*

Delusion of the day

Apparently, businesses are scarcely cognizant of how megatrends affect their organization, as research by KPMG makes clear.[33] Today is all that matters.

In fact, employees are far more cognizant that the organization they work for is falling behind; 55 percent believe their employer is too slow in responding to a world in flux, and 41 percent think that decisions are not being made at the appropriate level. Roughly 37 percent are sure their organization lacks the flexibility to adequately respond to changed surroundings.[34]

Nowadays, the only way businesses can succeed is through an ability to constantly adapt to the outside world. *"Organizations need to have an open mind and be geared up for change. They need to be willing to re-invent parts of their very business,"* according to Shafiq Khan, Senior Vice President of Global E-commerce at Marriot International. To him, the greatest challenge is working with outdated systems and procedures, in an environment where fixed values are becoming increasingly rare. Furthermore, he states that the digital revolution is still in its early stages and that the best is yet to come.

And now for something completely different...

For businesses, it no longer matters whether you are better, faster or cheaper than the competition; you need to be willing to start doing something completely different. John Sculley told me about the time when he had just left Apple, in the early 1990s. George M.C. Fischer, one of his friends, had just made a move from Motorola to Kodak as CEO, and he asked Sculley to join him within the company, to share his thoughts on the technological developments Kodak would have to focus on. Sculley needed no time at all to articulate his advice: move everything into digital photography. *"We had been working on this at Apple and I saw that it had tremendous potential. So I told George, 'the future will be about taking photos instead of making photos.' He answered that he was aware of that himself, but that I could not even begin to understand how daunting it was to convince all the 'chemistry buffs' – highly intelligent professionals whose main focus was producing tangible photographic prints – to move away from all that was familiar to them. 'They are completely cut off from reality', George said."*

"I look to the future, because that is where I will be spending the rest of my life."
– GEORGE BURNS, ACTOR AND SCREENWRITER

Google Chief Technology Officer, Michele R. Weslander-Quaid, once worked for Kodak too. She recounted a similar tale of the Kodak culture. When digital photography emerged, Kodak refused to believe it could produce the same result as photographic film. It proved absolutely impossible to make senior management realize that technological developments would make the company business model obsolete.

Apparently, 'doing something different' proves an immense challenge for a great many organizations. Clayton M. Christensen, Harvard professor and entrepreneur, argues that financial reasons (the need to instantly define a return on investment) and a rigid company culture may often be the cause for businesses failing to reinvent themselves again.[35] As it turns out, it is extremely difficult to remain focused on and reserve sufficient energy for a new initiative in its embryonic state, particularly when it still has to prove successful, and even more so when it is perceived to be 'foreign to the industry'.

With a related glance back at Dutch history almost two centuries ago, one of my Twitter followers alerted me to the fact that the parliamentary Commission on the 'Desirability of the Iron Railway' deliberated for six years before submitting its positive advice. Sometime later, it was rejected,[36] almost unanimously, by the House of Representatives. Resistance to innovation is, it seems, a facet of all ages.

Organizations will find a future in organizing on spec: based on 'learned ignorance'. Those who succeed in developing the right culture and supporting it with the right tools will be able to create a platform of innovation, thus making employees more loyal and creative, and the organization as a whole more flexible and agile. A speedboat is born. Competition will shift from being related to products and services, to competing for attention where everyone is providing their very own unique product or service. Size will cease to matter, as such, when companies are able to appear larger than they actually are, thanks to technology, or to find an appropriate niche.

Summary
It is both individuals and their networks who are embracing technology and the ensuing change noticeably faster than most organizations – as is to be seen all around us. Epic companies we

could not have envisaged ever losing their relevance are crumbling before our very eyes. Information, trends and news spread like wildfire the world over, as consumers and citizens are increasingly interconnected. Last but not least, new services and products become household names overnight, the world over, courtesy of the internet and other media. Organizations are then urged to launch products and services at breakneck speed. As a result, innovation and more experiments are called for.

> "Ready? Aim, and fire! Planning is overrated. Whoever tries out the most things, will win."
> – TOM PETER, MANAGEMENT THINKER

Perhaps surprisingly, innovation has a wish list of its own. Three things: the right people, the right technology and the right company culture. The culture often proves to be the greatest headache of the three.

Putting technology to its proper use often hits a proverbial wall, when company culture comes into play. If the right culture is lacking, don't even bother. Evolving ecosystems, flexibility, and an opportunistic – in the good sense of the word – way of working together, with flights of fancy and sans boundaries, all these have their beginnings in company culture.

It is, therefore, within organizations where the most significant change of our time needs to unfold. We shall explore this at length in the Chapter 2.

2. Charting a new course

It happened during a veritable feast in lovely surroundings. There were 15 of us, HR-directors and myself, together to discuss 'the employee' and 'the organization' of today and tomorrow. I told them: "Speedboats are proactive, agile, look outside themselves, connected to a network, bring added value to the customer, citizen or co-worker, and never stop learning. This is in stark contrast to professionals and organizations who remain firmly anchored in the age of industry, they are the oil tankers." On the periphery of my vision, I could see one of the directors becoming more agitated by the second, wringing her napkin to virtual shreds. Finally she burst out: *"But Menno, I do notice speedboats like that within my organization, but in reality most of them are in the process of leaving our company! What am I supposed to do with the huge grey mass of leftovers, who are sluggish to the end and cling to the unions and the works council in resistance?"* The ensuing silence was deafening. Then one of the other diners posed the question: *"Is it possible those employees behave like that, based on how you treat them?"* This remark produced a heated debate, on the extent to which staff is conditioned by their work environment. On the way home, my mind wandered to my conversations with ... where everyone in the organization is regarded as talented.[1] Their winning formula is a strict entry selection, the involvement of co-workers in that very selection, the drawing up of crystal clear targets and results, and allowing people to make mistakes, provided they learn from them.

In Culture Shock, Will McInnes gives the advice to just once pretend that your employees are in fact volunteers who could decide to do something else every single day. If that were the case, how would you treat them? How would you make sure they wanted spend time at your company, day after day?

Flexibility: need and want

It is not that long ago, that steady jobs were de rigueur, and professionals made long-term commitments to an organization. Those very same professionals now feel an increasing need for flexibility and freedom. At the same time, they too find themselves being expected to adapt constantly to a new reality; each new projected has this effect, as does the becoming obsolete of their old job due to an altered business model, automation or outsourcing. In the words of Jeanne Meister, co-author of Workplace 2020 – a must-read if ever there was one – and former Chief Learning Officer at IT company Sun Microsystems: *"The next decade will usher in new companies and business models that may seem unimaginable today but that will dramatically change how we live, work, learn, communicate and play. Workers should be able to adapt to these changes in order to thrive in the 2020 workplace, where transparency, collaboration, personalization and hyper-connectivity will rule the day."*[2]

There is, however, also a significant group of professionals who find it hard to move along with the changing views of work, and what is expected of them. They tend to adopt more of a wait-and-see approach, or at times just plain stubbornness. A divide may very well appear between those professionals who are able, of their own accord, to take the leap into the 'new world' and those who are not ready or willing to do so, or who feel a lack of support from the organization they work for.

A Dutch case

At Cap Gemini, an example of this divide became apparent when board member Jeroen Versteeg appealed to senior staff to take a 10 to 30 percent pay cut. This would be a way to help younger staff move through the company. The alternative would be re-structuring the business, and then the senior staff would just have to see if they kept their jobs. According to Versteeg, there was a 'mismatch between what people earn and what they are capable of'. His suggestion produced a tsunami of criticism. The media and unions were unanimous in speaking of its disgrace, and several internet forums practically exploded in the ensuing controversy.

Though his timing may have been off the mark, just as his tone and motivation might well have been, this incident does lay bare what the main issue is in today's job market: the world in flux requires a different set of knowledge and skills than that which many professionals can provide.

Employment agency Yacht has researched this mismatch. With depressing results, too: 88 percent of companies polled responded that, if there were no laws to ensure job security, they would certainly let certain employees go. A mere 35 percent of managers felt they were assured of having precisely the required talent within the company. Conversely, the organizations themselves actually have but a scant view of what the future holds, in way of challenges. In turn, managers tend to find it complicated to carry their employees with them in future developments, and to explain what it is that are expected to do.[3]

Consultancy firm Deloitte has produced a series of reports called Shift Index, in which they state: *"Workers who learn to continuously upgrade their skills and harness technology will increase their productivity. Those who do not will stagnate. This dynamic creates highly skilled, highly productive workers that are increasingly in demand. Salaries for these high-performing workers will continue to grow, exerting pressure on organizations' bottom lines."*[5]

"The majority of offices are full of people who are not working. If they were to work at home, at least they need not pretend to be working."
– MATTHEW MULLEN, FOUNDER OF AUTOMATTIC AND DESIGNER OF, AMONG OTHERS, WORDPRESS[4]

This is a trend: more and more of production value is concentrated within a shrinking group of professionals. Whether or not 'old-school' organizations, so-called oil tankers, with their slightly outdated structures and rarely motivating culture, will succeed in retaining this group, remains to be seen – not to mention if they will be able to afford them, if they do succeed. As I mentioned before, the other side of the coin is what effect this will have on those who are unable to make the transition. How will they raise income, when there are fewer steady jobs than ever? How will they have any kind of job security, and will they be able to work freelance?

"A lot of the people who are finding themselves out of work, due to the increase in computerization, unfortunately lack the skills to fill the newly minted positions," according to HR Director of the Dutch Tempo-Team agency, Suzanne Jungjohann. *"At the moment we can hardly imagine it due to the recession, but talent scarcity will truly be a huge problem that our economy will face in the next few years. Many job seekers will simply not be able to work, because of having the wrong profile. Business that fail to fill their vacancies, will poach employees from elsewhere. A war on talent, so to speak."*[7] According to employment agencies, the specializations which are much in demand are often in relatively new areas of expertise, such as data-analysis (big data) and 3D-printing. Job growth is mainly occurring at the top of the market, whilst for middle-level school-leavers there are in fact fewer jobs.[8]

> **"To a talented 'techie', what are the benefits of working from 9 to 5 as a manager? He would be better of designing his own app, right?"**
> – RICARDO SEMLER, CEO OF SEMCO[6]

The sensation of becoming obsolete overnight can be profoundly disturbing. A school principal acquaintance of mine once described to me how one of his teachers appeared before him one morning, on the verge of tears. Having always been the Apple expert of the school, now he suddenly – just three years before retiring – had to face a fifteen-year-old who was far more adept on a Mac than he. According to the principal, this teacher felt so totally obsolete, that he was ready to take early retirement that very day. The principal had to spend ages persuading him to allow the fifteen-year-old to assist him in his classes instead.

HEROs and HIPPOs

We shall continue to see more of these kinds of creative solutions and new working patterns. In *Empowered*, Josh Bernoff and Ted Schadler introduced the term 'HEROs' for Highly Empowered & Resourceful Operatives, professionals who, through adopting a new way of working (together) and cleverly utilizing digital technology, succeed in mobilizing powerful informal networks in order to do their work more efficiently and more enjoyably too. They are diametrically opposed to the HiPPOs, of the Highest Paid Person's Opinion. Forbes.com provides the best definition for this group: *"HiPPOs are leaders who are so self-assured that they need neither other's ideas nor data to affirm the correctness of their instinctual beliefs. Relying on their experience and smarts, they are quick to shoot down contradictory positions and dismissive of underling's input."*[9]

HEROs tap into the new era, or may even be the ones to shape it. HiPPOs resist developments, consciously or inadvertently, but this may in fact be a huge boost to the new developments. In the end, then, HEROs will transform structures from the ground up, which will prove to be a long and painful process. Many of them will not have the stomach to stick with their organizations, and instead end up turning their backs on them. HiPPOs 'with chutzpah' will realize that they cannot halt this development, and decide to adjust the relevant structures in such a way that the HEROs will feel at home after all.

A new way of looking at work

Jody Greenstone, founder and CEO of Business Talent Group, and Matt Miller, columnist for *The Washington Post,* believe a whole new class of workers is on its way: ones who bring added value in short-term jobs, and whose work is organized in projects. Working in temporary teams needs to be adopted and facilitated by organizations; otherwise they will not have access to this talented group. Greenstone regards knowledge work as being about 'the production of decisions'. Knowledge and knowledge workers are not inextricably linked; after all, knowledge may be shared.[10] It is of far greater importance to organizations that they interpret knowledge in a timely and precise fashion, and that they are sufficiently agile to come to the right decisions. An increasing number of organizations is therefore correct in opting for flexible, varying teams which are implemented as need be.

Sharing versus protecting

The very foundation of our new economy is made up of knowledge and its being shared through online networks. Building up one's network, maintaining and expanding it is what will be the core business for all of us. No longer owned by one person, knowledge will exist within the network, and its value will be measured by how you harvest the knowledge, adding to it and passing it around. Sharing knowledge has become a surer way to power than protecting it, which was the way of treating information in the past. You should never underestimate the power of collective wisdom.

> "No one is interested in all that you know; what matters is what you do, with your knowledge."
> – TONY WAGNER, INNOVATION AND TECHNOLOGY FELLOW AT THE HARVARD TECHNOLOGY & ENTREPRENEURSHIP CENTER

Professor Eric Tsui works at Hong Kong Polytechnic University and specializes in knowledge management. He told me how Japanese companies, like Honda and Toyota, often give their employees a different job five years before they retire, preferably outside their own department, in order to make sure their knowledge is transferred to co-workers.

For the most part, technology enables knowledge work to be done absolutely anywhere in the world. PowerPoints can be made up in India at a fraction of the cost of the Netherlands or other European countries. This does, however, have a downside: countless freelancers offer their services on so-called crowd-working networks. This may well be interesting for businesses, but at the Harvard Berkman Center for Internet and Society, co-founder Jonathan Zittrain warns us that these networks can best be regarded as 'digital sweatshops'.[11] After all, how will freelancers be affected, if their work is done in countries with a lower standard of living, and consequently far lower hourly wages?

Automated knowledge work

We are still in the earliest stages of a development; that is what we must realize. Not only will production work be automated, but knowledge work will as well. The way we do our work will be hugely impacted by this. A 'mobile' employee already checks their smartphone 150 times a day. Each check takes roughly 30 seconds. Just imagine what huge strides Google Glass and similar innovations could produce in terms of time saved.[12] And what will happen when we no longer need to don ridiculous glasses, but have all the required data freely available through our e-lenses?[13]

Transition into different ways of working and organizing

We need to stop thinking about work based on the industrial age model. This model is made up of a more or less fixed output, divided into several fixed working days, produced by a fixed number of employees. Instead we will start to work with more of a 'hybrid' model, where the make-up of work and employees is increasingly varied. This viewpoint is still for the most part completely opposite to the way we currently organize work. In the midst of a project, many employees are under huge pressure, particularly if they are involved in several projects at once. When the projects are drawing to a close, or conversely, when they are just getting started, there could well be a lull. Expensive professionals end up sorting through the archives, or sitting around surfing the internet. Why on earth should an organization not ask them to take their holiday at that very time, or even temporarily release them from employment, which would in turn produce significant savings on the salary costs. Naturally, this would have a profound impact on how we regard terms of employment.

I discussed these developments and challenges with Jimmy Maymann, CEO of *The Huffington Post*, arguably one of the most successful global online media brands. According to Maymann, news media – similar to scores of other organizations – have to deal with frequently conservative employees, who have held the same position for twenty-odd years. Maymann argues that old-school organizations are often full of countless managers, and in the transition from the age of industry to the network era, they are precisely the ones who lose their power. These people all need to step out of their comfort zone, which is easier said than done. For the news hacks of old, instead of simply writing a good article, there is a sudden need to interact with the reader – they have to respond to readers' reactions, optimize the article based on feedback – and maybe even make a video journal. This is a whole different ball game to handing in a finished article to the editor. It requires different skills entirely. *"The more traditionally minded media held onto the idea that the internet would prove to be a passing hype. We have now started many partnerships with traditional media, like Le Monde International, and it is precisely then that we notice how tough the new world is for them. For that specific reason, they relish working with us and adopting best practices for their own preferred media brands,"* Maymann ontinues.

Flexible shell

In looking at the statistics, you will find that the Netherlands has yet to successfully complete the transition to the more flexible model of work. The average term of employment is still roughly a decade; a percentage which has been relatively stable for the past fifteen years. Older employees in fact have an even higher average term of twenty years. It is worth mentioning that there are significant variations according to type of job; for support staff in finance, secretarial and HR the average is markedly lower. Only 4.7 percent of these workers have terms of employment that exceed ten years.

It is highly likely that the 'flexible shell' will double in size.

Currently, 10.9 percent is self-employed; whereas in 2040 this percentage will probably have grown to 20 percent.[14] *"Younger people are self-employed because they feel an intrinsic motivation to do so. They are focused on having fun and are less interested in how much they earn. Being self-employed allows them to work for numerous organizations in a short period of time and learn a lot in the process,"* according to Han Mesters, Business Banking Services Division at ABN Amro.[15] Mesters expects the flexible shell to grow in significance for businesses. *"Increasingly, they approach self-employed professionals directly and they use online communities to find the right people more than ever. Even in the current job market, they do not want a permanent position. This may well turn into a serious worry,"* Mesters remarks. *"For instance, it concerns financial specialists, certain IT fields, engineers, econometrists and actuaries."*

Ricardo Semler, the famous entrepreneur and management guru, is another huge fan of organizations having a considerable flexible shell. In the 1980s, Semler took over Semco as a business from his father, and over time made drastic changes to the organization, all of which were focused on creating more enjoyment at work for his employees. Semler got rid of most of the managers, allowed the staff to choose the board of directors and let them set their own salary. The company has certainly not suffered under this regime; the annual turnover is currently several hundred million dollars.

"Our generation wanted nothing more than to become CEO: move on up in the hierarchy, regardless of cost. If I were to be given the chance to do it again, I could absolutely care less. I do my best work when I can be creative; I excel at working with ideas. Let someone else run a huge organization like this. Thirty years ago, people would have thought you had lost your mind. Now we live in a global world and you can see an enormous amount of talent, incidentally outside those same huge organizations, more often than not."
– JOHN SCULLEY, FORMER APPLE CEO

Semler believes a business should have 70 to 80 percent of its employees through temporary contracts: *"When you open a factory, the odds are you will see a decline in sales after a few years. Products, people, talent; all of those are available on a temporary basis,"* said Semler, during one of his infrequent public events in the Netherlands. *"People who decide the company strategy should be retained for the long-term, as that is too complicated a job for someone from the outside. The same applies for employees who excel at technology or marketing, for instance. They are rare gems."*[16]

Flexible employment contracts, as argued for by people like Semler, are just the beginning. I believe that, in the future, positions will take on a far more dynamic nature. In a network era, there are simply endless ways to contribute, outside the realm of carved-out roles. In reality, job titles and descriptions are obstacles in the flow of knowledge, experiences and contacts. If we can break down those barriers, we shall succeed in building organizations with greater efficiency and employees may well find more inspiration in their work than they are able to in the current structure.

> **"Talented people no longer fit into well-defined positions."**
> – ANNEMIEKE ROOBEEK,
> PROFESSOR OF STRATEGY AND
> TRANSFORMATION MANAGEMENT

This change is already perceptible in several industries. The S100 – by their own account, an 'inter-university center for organization, change, renewal and leadership' – wrote on the 'five game-changers' for consulting, in their report: *"Consultancy firms are finding it increasingly hard to attract talented staff. In the pre-internet era, if you wished to be a consultant, joining a consultancy firm was the only way to go. Agencies possessed the networks, after all, and the client contacts. The arrival of internet and particularly of LinkedIn, has undercut the monopoly held by agencies. Any consultant worth his salt can use the internet to find out who is operating in the field he wishes to consult on. Proceeding to contact those clients directly is the next step. Furthermore, experienced consultants find there is little left to learn at organi-*

zations with traditional set-ups, so there are very few advantages to working for a consultancy firm. Increasingly, this means consultancy firms feel the competition from other businesses, like start-ups. The smartest graduates often find working at a start-up more appealing than joining a top consultancy; more excitement, less hierarchy, no endless slogging on the partner track, more enterprising and, to top it all off, more useful skills to acquire for the future."

Developing qualities of excellence

Lynda Gratton, author, consultant and Professor of Management Practice at the London Business School, is a prolific writer on the future of work. She believes today's era requires 'serial craftsmanship'. In other words: you can no longer afford to think your specialty will remain valuable all through your career, particularly if you bear in mind that many of us shall be working until our seventies. Professionals, then, will require ongoing schooling and training and, ideally, ought to acquire skills in several fields, and if they choose areas which are hard to outsource or computerize, so much the better.

Another way to distinguish oneself from the pack is to fuse various talents together. Become a professional blogger, content collector and curator, or social network analyst: these are all jobs where creative shaping, curating, culling, adding on, filtering and sharing information are all key. In fact, plenty of people have started to do this already – just look at the rampant growth of tools like Pinterest – though it is often treated as something 'on the side'. I keep coming across people who have this highly creative life outside their work. They are, in truth, displaying the skills they possess, skills which are generally hidden from sight, in their official job description, and which are not put to use there. If you pay close attention and ask

> **"Regardless of whether you want to pick up a new skill, or simply improve in your current job, you are now responsible for investing in yourself."**
> – REID HOFFMANN, CO-FOUNDER OF LINKEDIN, IN *THE START-UP OF YOU.*

the right questions, you will notice this very creativity in yourself and your co-workers. What is needed now is to fire up and tap into this creative spirit.

Robots

In the introduction, I mentioned the trend of our work increasingly being done by software and robots. Philip Parker, a professor at INSEAD, has written over one million books. That is to say, he has developed software which can independently (using highly complex algorithms) source articles and studies on a specific topic, analyze them, collate them, and put them into a readable and logical sequence. This with absolutely no need for a human author.[17] The program, which is called 'Lsjbot', currently writes 8.5 percent of all Wikipedia articles: just under three million entries.[18] There is no better way to illustrate the speed at which this development is rushing by.

Author and futurist Ross Dawson confirms this trend, and makes a point of emphasizing that people will need to give a different meaning to their work: *"As computers transcend many human capabilities and work is dehumanized, we must focus on the skills and abilities where humans excel beyond any imaginable machine capability. At the heart of those human capabilities are creativity and innovation."*[19] In his classic book, *The Rise of the Creative Class*, Richard Florida described human creativity as the ultimate economic raw material. So too does Gerd Leonhard, a self-confessed futurist' believe this era to revolve around the 'human factor': *"If our work, our output, is 'mechanical' and 'standardized', we will soon be overtaken by intelligent software and machines."*[20] The real question is whether or not we have a clear picture of which work can and cannot be automated in the near future. Technology may well be moving faster, and with greater impact, than we are able to imagine right now.

Clinging to the familiar

There is another problem. In absolute terms, there is a case to be made for more passion and creativity, but that does lay bare an uncomfortable truth, which is that not everyone is cut out for those things. A wide range of research has made clear that a serious proportion of employees are passive or have even mentally 'checked out' entirely.[21] It might seem undoable to incite this group of people to creative and innovative behavior. Now more than ever there is a huge challenge and, consequently, a responsibility for many organizations' management, to aid people who have difficulty keeping up on their transition to meaningful and fulfilling work. To be sure, employees shoulder part of that responsibility, but they are often at a loss for where to begin. Insecurity caused by their constantly changing surroundings will lead them to cling to the work they are used to. Even though this reaction is perfectly natural, it is by no means helpful. And this is why management has such a crucial role to play in this time of transition.

Enjoying yourself is one third

Some people say that their salary is all that matters. I do not believe that for a second. You can divide your life into three chunks: one third is sleep, a third is your personal life – where you can do what you like – and the final third is made up by your work. Sometimes that chunk grows in size, if you give up some sleep or personal time. But imagine how sad it would be if you only enjoyed one third of your life. I am sure you are able to list numerous obstacles which mean you cannot be creative or passionate until you are home, but how can you accept one third of your life being a complete and utter waste? Life is short, so you would be better off doing something you enjoy.

Detachment

Quite frequently, organizations are apparently not at all geared up for mobilizing professionals or letting them continue to study. In fact, all too often, further training is regarded as a luxury, a coveted extra for which you had better be grateful, a privilege to be earned, and which is therefore only granted to a chosen few within the organization.

Professionals who are impatient with organizations which cannot yet deal with this new way of investing in their staff will inevitably seek out ways to keep up on their own, and to continue to 'renew' themselves. The advent of the internet has after all brought infinite possibilities for this. Why should a car mechanic sit around waiting to be allowed to go on a vocational course, when there are all sorts of online tutorials? Your imagination is the only limit to what you can learn to do. If your boss will not 'allow' you to attend a conference, why not follow the conference on Twitter or through a live stream?

A while ago, my wife resigned from her managerial position and set up her own business. She decided to continue working as a freelance HR-consultant, so that she would not lose touch with her field, and in addition to that, she took an interior design course. When she wanted to learn Photoshop, she signed up for an online course through Lynda.com, a website which provides all sorts of courses, for the price of a very reasonable annual subscription. Since 2008 Lynda.com has had an annual growth rate of 42 percent.[22]

Vicious circle

Now that organizations are no longer required to meet their employees' training needs, a shift is occurring in the loyalty of professionals: they are now more loyal to each other and to their networks, than they are to the organization. Were this trend to continue, organizations would be increasingly less likely to invest in the teaching and training of their staff who, after all, may leave at short notice. This does, however inadvertently, rather feed on the employees' sense of detachment. A vicious circle is then born; with all sorts of fallout effects. In 2013, Yahoo spent roughly 200 million dollars on acquiring businesses, to recruit talented staff for one of its divisions.[23] Evidently, they were unable to find the requisite knowledge and skills in their existing pool of staff, and instead of opting for training, they decided to recruit new staff by means of takeovers.

> Reach out to your role models. Regardless of whether you are a carpenter, executive assistant or lawyer, role models are always around. You may know them personally; a co-worker with more experience,

the person who helped you at the outset of your career and left an unforgettable impression, or maybe a very young person, who brings new insights and skills with him. They might be people you find through LinkedIn or Twitter, or another online network. Involve them in your development; ask them for help or advice.

A professional I know has surrounded herself with a 'Board of Advisors'. She invited various people whom she believed would provide her with good advice. They became her 'shareholders' and at the annual 'shareholder meeting', they offered her all manner of advice on how to further her personal development in her career. Highly experienced men and women were gratified to share their knowledge at no charge whatsoever. Why? Because they were personally invited to do so, were acknowledged for their experience, and because they believed in the authentic narrative told by that particular enthusiastic woman.[24]

From process to pattern

Douglas Rushkoff describes the significance of 'creatives' in *Present Shock: When Everything Happens Now*. He believes that 'patterns' outdo 'processes' in degree of importance, in a highly complex and interconnected world. People with a creative mind are particularly adept at discerning patterns in a gluttonous soup of information. Rushkoff feels it would be wise to let children achieve these skills very early in life, by having them learn how to do programming, for instance. That would be helpful to them anyway, in a world where a great many things are programmed. Digital technology already makes up a large chunk of our lives, and that is by no means shrinking. By the year 2020 we are expected to be surrounded by some 26 billion objects – which just so happen to all be connected to each other – ranging from waste bins to lighting, kitchen appliances, moving vehicles and medical equipment.[25]

Skills which cannot be automated

Then, such skills as creativity and compassion, which we currently regard as pleasing benefits, will prove to be indispensable.

There will always be someone who knows more than you do; what will matter, however, is what you *do* with that information. This will make it far more important to increase your creative ability and degree of empathy. Even though you may not have the required knowledge yourself, you may well *know* someone with that knowledge, or otherwise you will be able to quickly track them down in your extensive network.

Consequently, professionals and managers need to be constantly reinventing themselves and putting as much initiative, passion and creativity into their work as they can. The best way to develop ourselves is along one of these three pathways:

- At a creative or strategic level, where your knowledge and inventiveness cannot be automated. These are the professionals who can shape the creative ability of an organization, who decide the strategy and/or watch over the vision and mission.
- In hyper-specialized work. These are the professionals who excel at one or more areas of expertise, or skills.
- As skilled workers such as carpenters, nurses, hair stylists, and so on.[26] These are people whose work is supremely local, or have an occupation where having a personal connection to their customers is key.

A new part for organizations to play

The key for successful businesses in the future is this: organizations ought to offer as much support as possible to these new professionals. Professor Henk Volberda defines 3M, Xerox and Southwest Airlines as companies which are innovative in this respect. Their staff does not consist of traditional workers who do their job according to a set 'job description', or within a fixed (often compartmentalized) team or department. Instead, they facilitate knowledge workers who are capable of developing new combinations of products and services. Those staff members have organized their surroundings in such a fashion as to offer the maximum in conducive contribution toward the achievement of their goals. They pay scant attention to structures, agreements and separate tasks, opting to offer a contribution to anything they feel would most benefit from it.[27]

Social innovation will make the difference

In a traditional structure, managers have no choice but to work with the qualities provided by their regular team. This lack of flexibility means they are losing the ability to adequately respond to the changing requirements they are faced with.[28] In order to be of interest to the talented staffers of the future, organizations will need to make adjustments to their structure, their method of collaboration and their management style.

Social innovation is in fact a rejuvenation of how work is organized within companies, in such a manner that both the productivity and the quality of labor benefit from it. The term 'social innovation' was coined to differentiate from the traditional term 'innovation', which generally refers to innovations in technology.[29] Way back, in 2004, Mike Johnson wrote these words in *New Rules of Engagement*: *"The ability to reach the hearts of workers, to have their goals and the organization's merge that will prove one of the greatest challenges of the next decade."*[30]

From the research of Henk Volberda, it is obvious that the lion's share (roughly three-quarters) of innovation is decided by how the conceived innovations are organized; which is to say, social innovation. Activities devised by R&D and purchased innovations, in fact, make up but a tiny sliver of innovative contributions to an organization's success. Certainly, technological innovation is a crucial 'ingredient', but he is convinced that the true acceleration and implementation are directed by social innovation.[31] He has outlined a number of significant prerequisites:

a) Creativity is brought to life through self-organization and cross-positional teams; i.e. teams made up of people who bring together a range of skills and knowledge.
b) Close-knit social networks of staffers, operating in decentralized cross-positional teams, provide space, ambition and enthusiasm.
c) The attitude of the management team is crucial to innovative success, not merely due to portraying a clear and challenging vision, but to encourage internal collaboration and sharing of knowledge.
d) Developing talent and rewarding teams produces extra efforts, the sharing of knowledge and the achieving of shared goals. In order to speed up processes of innovation, employee relations need to be geared to the ongoing development of talent, teamwork and rewards based on team achievements.
e) Innovation does call for working together with clients, suppliers and educational institutions.
f) The most innovative organizations are well aware of their strengths, *and* their weaknesses. Strengths are nourished and weaknesses are complimented by working together with other businesses and with educational institutions.

Summary

A wind of change is blowing through organizations, unsettling how work is organized, how professionals develop and even the very structure of organizations themselves. Creative pioneers have a bright future ahead of them. Smart professionals should then build on their creative strengths and further their specialist knowledge. Success and the ability to accurately handle information have become inseparable: information is to be gathered, filtered, curated and shared. Rather than scooping up as much information as you can find (anyone will tell you that software is far better equipped to do so), the secret is to become more 'human'. How to do so? By joining forces with other people, innovating current products and services, or even by going back to the proverbial drawing board, to develop entirely new ones.

3. From oil tanker to speedboat

It took a while but I am slowly getting to know them, these men and women standing at the helm of the start-up they launched either on their own or with a handful of companions. Nerds they are, in the nicest possible way, of course, but nerds. Their technological knowhow and skillset is blended with an unassuming modesty, a dash of wait-and-see and, often, even a shot of shyness. You might well expect to find an extrovert entrepreneur behind the wheel of a speedboat, but usually the opposite is true. This was brought home to me again during my visit to San Francisco and Silicon Valley, the epicenter of the digital revolution.

In a hip, edgy district of San Francisco, I meet up with Lukas Biewald, one of the founders of Crowdflower, the crowdworking platform. True to the start-up tradition, their office is really hard to find. An anonymous door opens onto a staircase up to a large office space above some shop or other, covered in plants towering up to the ceiling. Biewald fancies stretching his legs, and suggests we do the interview over lunch. My trip will not be complete, he urges, without having sampled the local meatballs.

The good ship – or speedboat rather – Crowdflower is sailing, as it were, on the waves of the trends discussed in previous chapters. It offers such organizations as Google, Apple, Instagram, Microsoft and Unilever access to a worldwide network of 'virtual workers. Literally millions of workers from more than 200 countries have together completed over a billion assignments for these clients. Unilever, for example, mobilized a small army of virtual workers to track consumers' online responses to the launch of their Dove Men+Care line. A good many companies do this by using software, but humans have proven to be much better in picking up the nuances in such feedback.[1] That's quite a relief – it shows yet again that we shall always need a human element in the way we work.

Biewald dreamt up Crowdflower long before crowdsourcing went hip, while he was working as a data scientist at Yahoo. There he noticed that when some jobs needed many extra hands on deck, the company tended to engage an outsourcing agency. 'There has to be an easier way,' thought Biewald. He announced such assignments online, thus arranging virtual labor for Yahoo. It turned out to be so easy to recruit people, and it delivered so much value added, that he soon saw that this could be a viable business model. When he started Crowdflower late in 2007, it was an overnight success. Its fast growth is, Biewald claims, still rather modest by Silicon Valley norms. So far, venture capitalists have invested a solid 13 million euros in the small company with its fifty-odd staffers.

Is it exploitation?
The concept of crowdworking networks such as Crowdflower has also come under fire.[2] In the previous chapter we saw how this way of working could be criticized as a 'virtual sweatshop'. The question clearly arises whether the use of virtual workers from countries with significantly lower rates of pay is not creating a situation where there are massive profits for such parties as Crowdflower, but only minimal returns for the workers.

The hallmarks of speedboats
Conventional thinking[3] once held that a business strategy should be implemented in one of three ways: operational excellence (low costs), constant innovation or by being completely customer-focused. Innovation was dealt with in a separate department, where it took years and years for anything to emerge. All of

that has totally changed. The rate of change is now many times higher, innovation is the name of the game on all fronts and new businesses – the speedboats – have change and innovation entwined throughout their organizational DNA. New entrants of the likes of Uber, Netflix, Airbnb en Zappos are active in each of the three strategic areas above. Their online platform and distribution facilities mean they have a very low cost level; they are constantly preparing and engaging in innovation and they are really accessible for the client; often precisely through their small and compact organization. Where once the challenge was to select which focus to go for, now it is in creatively getting everyone to combine all three.

Why is it that some people just keep heading down well-trodden paths, whilst others come up with an innovative idea? How can we characterize the thinking and the deeds of those people and companies whom I call 'speedboat'? In fact, they are really easy to define, since speedboats display remarkably similar behavior:

- They are extremely proactive
- They can transcend the traditional boundaries of organizations and markets
- They see (apparent) chaos as an opportunity. Their thinking is more cyclical than linear, and this is reflected in how they set up and manage their business
- They work with a provisional business model, which is flexible and adaptable when necessary
- Passion and the delivery of maximum added value are core values. The business facilitates staff to show this, and subordinates itself to this end.
- Their focus is most definitely external: they know full well what is happening in the world
- Anything which is not core is contracted out to networks
- All workflows, goals and results are public. This transparency gives staff the insights and overview they need to organize themselves.
- With such self-organization, there is little need for managers
- There is a prevalent culture of informality, with a good deal

of attention to forming and to maintaining this culture and context.

All these threads woven together fit a company such as Crowdflower as no other: the concept is supremely scalable. Everything is automated, so once the system is functioning well, it is easy to roll it out in other countries or to adapt it to different customers. Nowadays, Crowdflower works primarily with large companies, but Biewald also sees openings for a platform targeting small businesses and freelancers.

Not someone given to endless yakking, Biewald surprisingly opens up when he explains just how much Crowdflower is part of contemporary social evolution: *"There is undeniably a trend underway from the permanent to more flexible work relations. The idea that you have a regular job for a long while will increasingly fade into the background. The working environment will become ever more transparent, shaped by the relentless process of digitization. Your next job will come on the back of your last one, and thanks to metadata it will be possible to better measure the quality of your skills. Who knows, perhaps LinkedIn will one day add a 'Crowdflower rating' so that potential clients can see just how well you performed in earlier assignments."*

Transcending physical and organizational boundaries

Authors Yves Doz, José Santos and Peter Williamson introduced the term 'metanational' in their book *From Global to Metanational*. They believe that, in the past, you were able to succeed in becoming a global player, through market penetration the world over, with self-designed and often generic products and services. Now the 21st century is upon us, and innovation through learning from the world has become absolutely essential. Speedboat organizations possess three invaluable characteristics:
• They have the ability to be the first in identifying new technology and knowledge, anywhere in the world, and subsequently put it to use
• They have the ability to harness global knowledge and then

channel it into new products and services, outsmarting their competitors in the process

- They have the ability to globally monetize this innovation

If being one of the speedboats is your business goal, then you ought to create a network of pioneers to stay abreast of new trends and developments. The next step is to build the right structure and, more importantly, the right culture, in order to translate new trends and new knowledge into new product market combinations. You should have the ability to collect fragmented knowledge from within the organization and proceed to focus it on the desired innovation. Scott Klososky comes up with the term 'geek seeding' in his book *The Velocity Manifesto*: identifying technology-based talent within the company and giving these people strategic positions. It can be especially useful to do this for positions where you would not expect to come across a person from a technology background, i.e. supplementing the HR department with a data analyst, or having a web designer sit in on strategy meetings for a new business model.

Thrive on chaos

At first glance, unstructured chaotic systems may not produce the results that tightly organized structures do. They are, however, far more valuable. At times, this even takes on a literal sense, as apparently is the case with the physician and micro-biologist Alexander Fleming. He had just such a disjointed workflow, and that it is often credited as being the factor leading to hisdiscovery of antibiotics. Similarly, Charles Goodyear accidentally stumbled upon the method for vulcanizing rubber – an important part of the process involved in making rubber tires – when he let a pan of mixed rubber boil over on the hob, in one of his chaotic moods. [4]

Flexible business models

Increasingly, large companies are being left behind. The Indian ICT titan Tata Consultancy Services noticed their software packages, which involved the work of literally hundreds of staff members, being overtaken by countless apps conquering part of the market for software. To be sure, apps are partial solutions, but the very second a platform is able to link an end user's apps together, it may well be curtains for the traditional approach favored by Tata. Chief Financial Officer Rajesh Gopinthan insists his company is shifting its focus from a mere handful of large and complex software solutions to hundreds of modular apps. In so doing, the organization is increasing its agility and becoming more tuned in to the rapid market changes.[5] Tata have realized the need for being supremely outwardly focused and having a flexible business plan. This approach requires a particular kind of person, who is not necessarily available to every company out there. If this person is indeed missing, then business can resort to the approach opted for by Facebook: simply acquire the most successful start-up. Facebook took over WhatsApp for 19 billion dollars in 2014.[6] At that point, the start-up had been in business for five years, had a staff of fifty people and nearly 500 million users.[7] This miniature global player had succeeded in bringing down virtually all the giants in the telecom industry. *"Looking back, telecom ought to have designed a joint chat service,"* according to Marco Kind, T-Mobile CCO of Consumer Business. Vodafone Product Marketing Manager, Jan Jongeneel, echoes this sentiment in saying: *"Innovation has been sorely lacking in the field of* 'messaging'. *After all, for years text messages provided an easy source of income."*[8]

Delivering passion and value added

The telecom provider known as 'giffgaff'– named after the Scottish Gaelic term for 'mutual giving' – is another prime example of a speedboat. It operates in the UK market. Not a stand-alone company, it is in fact part of the Telefónica Group, making it a speedboat next to an oil tanker. Customers are the key to giffgaff, or to be more precise, customers effectively run the company. In point of fact, I am not allowed to call them 'customers', as giffgaff prefers the term 'members'. During my visit to the London office, CEO Mike Fairman proudly showed me the horns which are present on the table in every single room. Anyone caught referring to the members as 'customers' has to endure the horn being tooted at them by co-workers: yet another instance of how well speedboats succeed at producing a culture of informality, where the company positively oozes its vision from its pores. 'Membership' is at the very core of giffgaff. The organization of the company is all done online, and the members fill the various positions within the company. Customer service, I beg your pardon, member service is provided by members who are particularly knowledgeable on a specific topic. The platform is provided by giffgaff but they have only a paltry fifty people on staff. Mind you, this is a business with well over a million members and an annual turnover of just under 100 million pound sterling. Virtually all the marketing is done through the program of members-recruiting-members. Additionally, members provide their own tutorial videos, apps, commercials and admin. So-called 'superusers' put in up to 170 hours a month for giffgaff, with no salary in return. Those hours are not solely for operational tasks, either, but for strategic input as well. Roughly ten thousand ideas for improving giffgaff's performance record were suggested through an innovation platform: suggestions for new price ranges, marketing campaigns, new business models and so on.[9] Almost four hundred of these have been put into effect. The members are rewarded with virtual credits, which can be exchanged for money or products.

Waxing lyrical, Mike Fairman says: *"More organizations ought to listen to their customers and actively engage them in conversation. Why on earth would you let people who are passionate about your product convene elsewhere? It makes it that much harder to communicate with them than if you do so in your own community. This model is conducive to a far smaller business model and a much greater degree of efficiency. In one fell swoop, you accomplish both a deeper involvement with your company and a reduction in costs. After all, most people enjoy helping others."*

"People don't buy what you do, they buy why you do it."
– SIMON SINEK

The giffgaff concept can be applied to a variety of businesses and markets. It truly makes the customer its first priority, instead of them just being a sentence in the mission statement. A prerequisite, however, is not to be too attached to your brand, your standing or position. You need to be willing to surrender power. Though it is of course still to be determined how much power you really have, anyway.

External focus

Jeff Bezos read an article in 1994 on the rise of the internet and the prediction it would become a global phenomenon, hugely impacting sales of all manner of products and services. Bezos decided to look for a product which he could sell easily through the internet and which would be simple to ship. He landed on books. He opted for Seattle as the place of business, partly due to the many computer programmers in residence and because of its proximity to a sizeable distribution point for books. Thus Amazon was born.[10]

One of speedboats' key characteristics is their ongoing re-invention through a commitment to learning. When I spoke with Christopher Lukezic, one of the first employees of Airbnb and currently their Head of Communication, he agreed with this description of character. He believes all disruptive businesses are perpetually focused on innovation. Problem solving is their middle name, and they focus on making life easier for their customers, through creative technological applications. When I ask him for a pertinent 'golden tip' for organizations, Lukezic says the focus should be on consumers' needs for today, rather than searching for an answer to what they may want in the future. *"Nobody knows what the needs will be of future consumers. In order to stay relevant, you will need to maximize your current connection with them and be prompt in meeting the needs they have right now. That is the best way to be able to meet their needs in the future as well."* This is why Airbnb, and practically any other new organization, awards a central role to learning.

Should innovation not stem from employees or customers,

then it will do so from other stakeholders, such as suppliers or even the competition. They do not conceive of boundaries between organizations, but instead choose to regard the market as an ecosystem, of which they are one of the parts. Bol.com and Amazon are organizations which allow other vendors onto their platform, and even facilitate individuals who wish to sell their second-hand books.[11] Zappos lets suppliers have access to its ordering system, so they can decide for themselves when to deliver new stock. All that needs to happen, then, is for a Zappos staffer to sign off on the order. In *Delivering Happiness*, Tony Hsieh says: "*The typical industry approach is to treat vendors like the enemy. Don't show them any respect, don't return their phone calls, make them wait for scheduled appointments, and make them buy the meals.*"

Conversely, Zappos operates on the understanding that if your suppliers are happy, this will be reflected in the quality of the service they provide you. If they are not being exploited, they will have sufficient funds for innovations, for example, or to improve the supply chain with; Zappos will ultimately reap the rewards from all of them.

Aircraft manufacturer Lockheed has a similar strategy. As an organization, it actively invests in improving the management and innovative ability of its thousands of suppliers. Lockheed does this, by sharing all kinds of information and insights, which could benefit the suppliers, through the online platform Supplier Wire.[12] There are webinars to be taken, chat sessions with company employees, and the sharing of experiences with other suppliers in online meetings.[13]

Besides, speedboats are extremely focused on the market and consumers. Unparalleled in their 'intuitive' understanding of the market, they leave no technological stones unturned. Some of them even succeed in operating like a kind of ecosystem. Amazon, for instance, has organized its bountiful supply into clever and clearly set out categories, all of which are made available to consumers in one convenient location. The company also has an exceptionally efficient method for supply management, runs the online crowdworking network Mechanical Turk, sells off excess space on its server (Amazon Web Services), and has recently entered the field of logistics through the use of drones. Apple has a similar wide range of activities: in creating iTunes, the iPod, followed by the iPhone and iPad, it has come up with a profusion of hardware, software and services. Building 'ecosystems' along this line of thinking calls for a radically different way of doing business.

The Economist ran an article on how oil tanker Wal-Mart felt 'inspired' by the success of speedboat Amazon and is now actively aiming for a self-described creation of 'market ecosystems': clustering a great variety of different activities in one huge proposition for the customer.[14] Now, superstores double up as distribution points for a range of new, small stores, which are supplied from there. In turn, these new and profoundly local branch stores are used as pick-up points for online purchases. This whole enterprise means literally and metaphorically shorter lines, through which the company is able to anticipate the ever-changing wishes of the consumer. The first tests of the 'ecosystem' have shown an impressive 35 percent growth in sales. Another feature Wal-Mart has copied from the Amazon strategy is to have outside vendors sell their wares through its online sales platform. This has brought the number of items on sale up to 5 million. Not surprisingly, this fresh focus on technology and logistics has led to the creation of a completely new position: 'Chief of E-commerce Logistics'.

Still, Wal-Mart is by no means out of the woods yet. In spite of an increase in online sales to ten billion[15], it is a number that evaporates when compared to the 170 billion dollar turnover realized by Alibaba.com, the Chinese counterpart of Amazon. They have done so partly as a result of adopting the

"Companies like Wal-Mart, these big-size buyers, killed a lot of SME buyers. But now most of the SME buyers and sellers started to do business throughout the world because of the internet. So I think the world has moved. I strongly believe small is beautiful."
– JACK MA, CHAIRMAN OF ALIBABA.COM [16]

same strategy as Amazon; by allowing other parties to use their platform for sales of their own products.[16] Founder and chairman, Jack Ma, firmly believes the difference between speedboats like his own company and Amazon, and oil tankers such as Wal-Mart, is to be recognized mainly in how they deal with technology. Speedboats see it – combined with an insatiable desire for the 'cutting-edge' – as an inseparable part of company culture.[17]

It is with good reason that the walls of the Amazon offices have these words on them: *"There's so much stuff that has yet to be invented. There's so much new that's going to happen."*[19] Without a doubt, Jeff Bezos had this motto on his mind, when he acquired *The Washington Post* in 2013.[20] Though you might have expected otherwise, Bezos had no clearly defined plan behind this huge purchase, as becomes obvious in reading a letter to his new employees: *"There is no map, and charting a path ahead will not be easy. We will need to invent, which means we will need to experiment."*[21] Luckily, Bezos is in a position to take ample time to design a new business model; his pockets are unfathomably deep.[22]

Oil tankers learn from speedboats

Increasingly, oil tankers are discerning the powers of the speedboat, and are trying to adopt their culture and frame of mind. One oil tanker that pops up is the Finnish company Sanoma, known for various online and print magazines, and websites including nu.nl, kieskeurig.nl and startpagina.nl. To become part of the new era, the company has established a separate entity to take part in outside start-ups, called Sanoma Ventures. In addition to this, so-called 'accelerators' have been set up as a way to stimulate new initiatives within the company. When I visit him at the Amsterdam office, Chief Strategy & Digital Officer, John Martin gushes: *"My goal is to have at least four new concepts up and running, which are equally successful as Nu.nl, in five years' time."* Martin firmly believes a hundred of small businesses need to be built, in order to reach those four successes. The vast majority is, consequently, destined to fail. Besides, in the pursuit of those one hundred, literally thousands of ideas need to be floated. *"We basically need a tsunami of concepts, to be successful,"* Martin concludes.

Cultural shift

In Martin's mind, a cultural shift – from being risk-averse to being enterprising, curious and willing to make mistakes – is crucial for this project to succeed. He has cut out a decisive role for himself, too: *"Within the company, I am the bridge between the traditional world and the new digital world. I am the youngest person on the board - a 'forty-something'. The next generation still lacks the seniority to shift the people who are currently in power."*

I probe Martin for the reason why Sanoma made such a monumental decision in charting this course. *"We are under attack from pirates, who are biting great hunks out of our business models, in all kinds of areas."* For years, the conglomerate has suffered losses through the declining sales of magazines and the collapse of the market for advertising.[23] In the interest of deflecting the attacks of (mostly online) new market players and bravely bearing a dwindling income, Sanoma has invested heavily in all digital developments. Not without its challenges, this is, for an organization whose bulk – 70 percent no less – is based on non-digital products, and which is hardly eloquent in its digital mind-set.

I noticed, in the arguments Martin used, that technology was a mere part of the narrative; the main focus is on adopting a new way of thinking about your products and services, as well as how you interact with your customers. A media company like Sanoma may well have to deal with a faster evolution than other industries; the focus first shifted from print to digital. And no sooner than media companies had caught up with this development, did it shift to mobile technology. In a pre-internet era, you could get away with continuously improving

> "We are simply hopeless at radical innovation. Corporate business often has a culture aimed at accountability. That is not the way to find the next Google."
> – ANTOINE HENDRIKX, INVESTMENT DIRECTOR OF SANOMA [24]

company procedures, but now everything revolves around new, innovative ideas. These ideas are not necessarily conceived at the top of a hierarchy, but rather deep within the organization. There needs to be an arena where people can bring their excellent plans, and this will involve the breaking down of any existing conventions.

A new role for the consumer

Getting his employees excited is what Martin is after; as is making them think about how to digitize the connection between the consumer and the existing content. At present, a large proportion of the staff are being trained in the 'Lean-Development' method, a way to produce innovations to products and services, in a rapid and intuitive fashion, while simultaneously making sure customer input is included from the outset. *"It may sound completely self-evident, but in the past – similar to many companies – we often spent two years on the development of new concepts, before the client was even involved. Now we experiment* together *with the client and we only continue building on something that actually triggers the customer."*

Spirit of enterprise

Sanoma initially planned to collect all digital activities in one separate department. In the end, this was not the best possible solution. Although it might have increased their agility and brought them 'closer to the market', it would have unfortunately complicated the upscaling and international launch of any initiatives. Martin: *"I was aiming for an increased 'spirit of enterprise'. That is why we set up the accelerators: they need to be built separately from the existing brands, yet leave the possibility open to integrate them at a later stage."*

Hence, Martin bundled people together from all over the organization: financial staff, HR employees, digital workers and even people from outside the company. They included students and employees from other organizations, such as KPN. From the outset, everyone involved aimed to take up a new perspective on the current procedures and patterns within and surrounding Sanoma. In particular they focused on mobile, content, commerce, video and learning. This way of operating should transform Sanoma into a learning, flexible and transparent organization.

Mutual strength

One of the first triumphs of this internal path towards new businesses is Fashionchick.nl. It is a great example of how the mutual strength works between a start-up and a large company. Fashionchick rides the waves of knowledge inside Sanoma – including how to channel traffic on a platform, and how to effectively reach a new and young target audience. This kind of hybrid model is the future, says Martin.

One of the advantages of oil tankers is that they have big data in their possession: all kinds of information about their customers. When Sanoma decides which start-ups to actually go into business with, they will make serious use of big data. Though Martin does acknowledge that big data being used is hugely daunting to many people, he believes that it can be extremely useful, too: *"Until recently, the creatives were in power, but that will not work in the new world. We need to and we shall, in fact, use big data to improve ourselves. The article which I wrote on this topic, 'Sexiest job at Sanoma: Data Scientist' was my best-read-ever blog post.[25] We have an immense presence in profoundly interesting 'ecosystems'. We may well have more access to our customers in those systems than Google or Facebook has. On average, we reach literally everybody at least once a week, in both Finland and the Netherlands. All these interactions produce a wealth of data. Currently, we only use a small portion of that, in order to manage our business models. All the information is stored in virtual 'silos', but once we succeed in liberating it from there, give it meaning and then hook it up to dashboards for our advertisers, the world will be our oyster. I would not be at all surprised, if we were to end up being a data company."*

Only do what you excel at

I ask Martin what he believes to be the biggest challenge on this journey. He offers a clear-cut answer: *"Pulling the plug on initia-*

tives will be hardest. Starting something is not easy either, but usually it ends up on its feet. Get the right people working on it, make sure they have the optimal facilities and you will see truly spectacular things happen. However, we are at risk of having a hundred start-ups at some point and not being ruthless enough in culling, which means they will not succeed in the long run, after all."

Martin believes start-ups need to be protected from engaging in non-essential tasks, which will lead them to lose focus of their goal. *"Right now, Nu.nl has one billion page views monthly, even though we almost pulled the plug on it, a few years back. What in fact proved to be the most effective move, was to strip back costs to the absolute minimum. Not until we had done so, did it really begin to take off."*

Keep on learning

In its 'TimeSpace' initiative, *The New York Times* is on the lookout for the value added that speedboats have to offer. It boils down to three different start-ups constantly having four months of free rent at the newspaper's office on 8th Avenue in New York. This way, the newbies get access to meet relevant *NYT* staffers and ask them for help in tweaking their products or services.

Of course, the start-ups come bearing virtual gifts too. According to Rajiv Pant, Chief Technology Officer, TimeSpace is the media player's attempt at keeping up with the world in flux. *"We are a business focused on providing high quality news and background coverage, and we aim to constantly use the best available instruments, in order to gather, enrich and distribute this information. Increasingly, we have reached the conclusion that we are unable to do this merely by utilizing the knowledge and experience we have on hand, within our company. To be explicit, there are cases where the existing experience actually slows us down and bears judgment on us, instead of bringing us further."*

The idea is to have a true exchange of ideas: it will provide *The New York Times* with an opportunity to find out how start-ups work. How are their ideas born; how do they develop their products and services; moreover, how do they build their business and work together? In turn, the start-ups gain access to the knowledge and experience of the established newspaper: *"Part of it is aimed at doing a good thing, and giving new businesses a chance. They can learn from us, about how it works in a bigger company. There is a lot of knowledge buzzing around us. They can also meet other companies through us, who may become future customers for them. It is a bold and innovative course of action, so we'll just have to see... Learning is simply something of enormous value, both in a formal educational setting and when people learn from each other,"* Pant concludes. This initiative has generated plenty of good publicity for *The New York Times*, which is an added bonus.

It is as an experiment, that TimeSpace is being emphatically introduced within *The New York Times*, mainly to keep high expectations at bay; Spanish Telefónica has started a similar project. The telecom company has built a network of 'incubators' for start-ups. In a mere two years, the company has invested a total of 9 million euros in 295 start-ups in Barcelona, São Paulo and Prague.[26] Conversely, Samsung opts for setting up its own 'innovation centers' in areas where there is already a higher than average concentration of start-ups, such as New York and Silicon Valley, rather than bringing the new businesses to them.[27] Governments have in fact jumped on the start-up bandwagon, and make attempts to join up with new businesses, in order to learn from each other. For example, the Dutch Embassy in Athens makes office space available to young Greek and Dutch entrepreneurs. In exchange for a peppercorn rent, they are coached by people from such businesses as Philips, KLM, FrieslandCampina and ABN Amro.[28]

Reservations

According to KPMG, growing a business's own strengths in innovation and competitiveness as well as utilizing the latest technological applications offered by start-ups, are the main reasons for big companies to collaborate with them. For the start-ups themselves, the key attraction is the perception that big businesses will enhance their chances of a successful launch of their product or service. So too do big companies prove helpful in further developing the start-ups and in accessing new and international markets. To be brief: the value added for the start-ups by the collaboration is that it can speed up their business.[29]

There are, however, some serious hurdles for a start-up to crash into: the amount of time it costs to access the right person, going through complicated risk, procurement and contract procedures, sluggishness and tedious decision making processes, a lack of transparency, all of which can lead to a lack of trust.

> **"If you score together, you start to love each other. You need an initial success, else the relationship will wither and die, because nothing has come of it."**
> – JEROEN VAN DER POEL, DIRECTOR OF BUSINESS DEVELOPMENT, G4S SECURE SOLUTIONS

On the other hand, big companies often have difficulty in scouting the most promising start-ups, and the ones best suited to their business. According to oil tankers, start-ups are far too involved in the development of their product or service and consequently not adequately involved in sales and the actual market. An added challenge can be that start-ups do not always pay sufficient attention to the scaling of their business model.

There are other reservations that one could come up with, too, with regard to this kind of initiative. Former Apple CEO, John Sculley, is in fact quite skeptical of initiatives like Time-Space. He believes start-ups prefer to remain at a safe distance from oil tankers, because in the event of collaboration or a takeover, they would suck the lifeblood out of the speedboat. Sculley says he can name but a few start-ups that have actually profited from this type of project.

Rife with obstacles, we may conclude: for large companies it can prove hard to seek out the relevant start-ups popping up, locally, nationwide or globally, not to mention reaching those start-ups that complement the strategic innovation needs of the company. During the stage of orientation, difficulties can arise from discerning which product or service the start-up has in fact developed, what the value added would be to the market and their own business, which stage of market and product development the start-up is at and what kind of quality the entrepreneurs behind the start-up actually have. Add to that the speed at which new developments currently pop up, and you will find one start-up's product being overtaken by an even more innovative version from another start-up.

> "I am convinced that many big businesses have yet to fully tap into the potential offered by collaborating with start-ups. Apparently, it is quite a challenge to discover what the most effective way to work together is."
> – DJEEVAN SCHIFERLI, BUSINESS DEVELOPMENT EXECUTIVE, IBM

Summary
Speedboats share a number of hallmarks:
- They are extremely proactive
- They can transcend the traditional boundaries of organizations and markets
- They see apparent chaos as an opportunity. Their thinking is more cyclical than linear, and this is reflected in how they set up and manage their business
- They work with a provisional business model, which is flexible and adaptable when necessary
- Passion and the delivery of maximum added value are core values. The business facilitates staff to show this, and subordinates itself to this end.
- Their focus is most definitely external: they know full well what is happening in the world
- Anything which is not core is contracted out to networks
- All workflows, goals and results are public. This transparency gives staff the insights and overview they need to organize themselves.
- There is barely any need for managers with such self-organization
- There is a prevalent culture of informality, with a good deal of attention to forming and to maintaining this culture and context.

Big businesses – oil tankers – want to learn from speedboats and therefore seek them out to collaborate with, be that by investing in them or perhaps temporarily bringing them into the company. This involves certain risks: both for the oil tankers and the speedboats, it can prove difficult to find a match that is mutually beneficial.

4. From speedboat to oil tanker

We set up the meeting by a tweet. *The Huffington Post* CEO, Jimmy Maymann, excels at approachability and is visibly pleased to make time for me. Before we step into his office – a tiny space, which barely fits the two of us (Maymann believes a large office just puts up barriers for people to talk to you) – he shows me around the new recording studio, which has been given pride of place in the large, open-plan and flexibly organized area.

The Huffington Post is one of the most successful media companies in the United States.[1] Arianna Huffington and Kenneth Lerer set up a liberally-minded political blog in 2005, which was named among *Time Magazine*'s most popular blogs in 2009.[2] One list even named *The Huffington Post* the most influential blog in the world.[3] In 2010 the online magazine was acquired by AOL for 315 million dollar.[4] Nowadays, *The Huffington Post* no longer writes about politics alone, and you would be hard-pressed to call it a mere blog, so wide is the range of media which the magazine utilizes to reach its target audience. It is precisely for that reason that I decided to approach Maymann for a chat.

Being a speedboat within an oil tanker

In 2011 Jimmy Maymann (Denmark, 1971) sold his six-year old business GoViral to AOL for just under a hundred million dollars. Instead of spending his life playing golf on a tropical island, he became CEO of *The Huffington Post* news platform after being asked to do so by none other than Arianna Huffington. *"I much prefer being active to lazing around on a beach all day,"* he says, and besides: *"If I am able to do interesting things, the odds are that I will stay, so that's why I am here today. It still feels like a start-up. The energy here is positively buzzing and the people working have kept their level of ambition. All that is very different to a normal, established business."*

However, Maymann does notice challenges in operating within a large organization: *"In your own company, you know everybody, you have created a particular culture and you reach decision quickly, and together. The speed at which you are able to anticipate market developments is extremely fast. In my position as CEO of* The Huffington Post, *I am dealing with a brand with its own established strength, and of which I was not a founding father. You jump onto a ship, which has left the harbor already. Not to mention the corporate owner, with a very strong brand of its own. Each brand and each company brings attendant procedures, more policy and more people involved whom you have to take into account."*

According to Maymann, understanding all the different positions and interests of those involved is one of his key learning experiences. One of the challenges he continues to face, is: *"How can we succeed in staying on course, with* The Huffington Post, *and simultaneously contribute to the goals and expectations of the other stakeholders?"*

Staying up to speed

Both Maymann himself and his boss Arianna Huffington are obviously successful at this balancing act, or so I gather from his tale. Maymann initially refused the offer of the CEO position. The corporate world held no appeal for him: too large, too unwieldy and political, not sufficiently innovative or enterprising. He was proved to be correct in that respect: even though AOL acquired *The Huffington Post* in order to possibly adopt its internal culture and innovative workflow, the very first thing they did was to centrally organize all manner of positions. Any enterprising talent was broken up and the previous 'uplifting' effect from all the passionate souls working on the blog disappeared too. Maymann made it very clear to Arianna Huffington, that, given the situation, he was unable to bring the company to the required level. In order to do so, he would need actual control over a range of positions, including HR, ICT and sales. In fact, Maymann made this into a condition of his accepting the position: *"If I were to join them, I was adamant that it be a stand-alone company. Sharing things is understandable, but I needed to be able to decide what was right for* The Huffington Post, *without taking into account what would be best for AOL. There had always been a culture of advancement, enterprise and innovation at* The Huffington Post, *and if we were careless, then the AOL conglomerate would slow us down, even though speed is a key component of our DNA."*

Tapping into power without relinquishing uniqueness

Maymann has ambitions, he wants to turn *The Huffington Post* into a global brand and he wants to do so unencumbered: *"I refuse to have to stand in line at AOL when I want to launch a new project. I want to decide those priorities with my own team. And we need to move quickly, and then, anything else becomes irrelevant."* On the other hand, he does admit to being made out of the same mold as managers at big companies, even though he has never lumped himself with the 'corporate guys'. Every single entrepreneur, no matter how innovative, is bound to discover at some point, that structure, planning and control are at least minimally necessary. I think Maymann particularly excels at 'managing complexity': he is an entrepreneur and, as such, can address the enterprising qualities of others, ensure the means are in place to pick up speed, but he possesses the required political antennae to keep the bigger picture in mind, too.

Without relinquishing the uniqueness of the speedboat, *The Huffington Post*, Maymann is endowed with the gift of harnessing AOL's oil tanker power to his advantage. That is quite a feat; after all, most speedboats have great difficulty in keeping their head above water in an established organization.

Introducing innovation at an oil tanker

When they acquire speedboats, a great many oil tankers have a hard time integrating the new ideas and people into the existing structure. So why do they even attempt to, anyway? The reason lies in their limited ability to innovate, which hampers most large businesses. They simply *have to* source their innovation from outside, however complicated that may be. Generally, while an oil tanker may succeed in identifying the right innovation, the real challenge is in actually embedding those actual ideas into the established organization.

The New York Times offered a senior staffer an executive position with the responsibility for the 'full customer experience'. He refused the offer, fine and challenging though it may be, because he expected the current journalists would not succeed in putting the reader first, particularly if this would involve a new approach to work.[5]

> "All too often, at *The New York Times,* an article is regarded as finished, when the writers and editors hit 'publish'. At *The Huffington Post,* the moment when we hit 'publish' is when the article's lifespan has only just begun."
>
> – PAUL BERRY, FORMER CTO AT *THE HUFFINGTON POST* [6]

Cultural shift

Realizing that the need for innovation is one thing, but being able to nudge the internal change procedure into motion, and getting everyone to join in is something else entirely. I have witnessed this struggle at many businesses, over the past two decades. In order to truly admit renewal, you need to be bold in questioning intangible entities such as culture and traditions. Frequently, apart from having been explicit for decades, workflows are in fact implicitly organized. All of a sudden, here are these people from outside the organization, who say: *"Forget everything you learned the past twenty-five years, we are going to do things differently from today onwards."* The status quo is inclined to hear that as: *"You have been doing everything wrong until now and, actually, you've been half-asleep besides."*

According to Google CTO, Michele R. Weslander-Quaid, only leaders who do not fear change and are not threatened by smarter individuals, can in fact succeed in guiding this process. They ought to realize that shared knowledge doubles the power, too.

My conversation with Jimmy Maymann continues, after he has wandered off to fetch both of us more coffee. He echoes the words of Michele R. Weslander-Quaid: *"Innovation often stems from people who refuse to be limited in their actions, who do not want to be held back by procedures and managers and who long to completely focus on their passion."* He has noticed that many innovative professionals and entrepreneurs never completed their degree. To his mind, this can be explained by how the educational system is set up, everybody learning the same topics in more or less the same fashion. That makes it hard to be creative: *"We have less difficulty in teaching people how to draw up a balance sheet, make a PowerPoint presentation or formula in Excel, than we do in teaching them to be creative and enterprising."*

Experiment

I would like Maymann to explain how he made 'experimenting' an essential part of *The Huffington Post*. One way to do so was the video channel HuffPost Live: *"On the one hand, there are parties like* The Guardian, *on the other there is Twitter. We wanted to combine those two polar opposites, through a participation platform. Creating our own source of news, and simultaneously letting people join in, giving them a voice of their own."*

To put it mildly, it has been quite successful. Sometimes the digital channel has over a million views a month.[7] HuffPost Live mainly focuses on a younger demographic that grew up with real-time communication and interaction. It is a completely new format, utilizing the creativity of the viewer. *"We discovered that the image quality is less important than what is in fact being said, and the subsequent discussion. Technology is merely a tool to give people a voice. The raw edges are precisely what give it an authentic feel."*

Flat organization

Setting up a start-up in a garage is actually not that difficult, nor is coming up with things like HuffPost Live. The actual difficulties rear their ugly heads once you become an organization of more than fifty people, as people keep finding out. Maymann says: *"From a staff of around fifty, you become a 'proper' company, which requires some kind of structure. I wish I could say we are completely unstructured, but we do have one, and in fact, there is nothing wrong with that. What may well be more significant is that we do not have a strict hierarchy, and we make it a priority to ensure our professionals have maximum interactions, both virtually and in person, regardless of their position or area of expertise."*

"As a leader, you need to be able to describe the desired outcome, not the road to reach that outcome; if you cannot, then you will remain stuck in today's dogma."
– MICHELE R. WESLANDER-QUAID, CHIEF TECHNOLOGY OFFICER AT GOOGLE

The realization of a flat organization like this, and facilitating mutual contact, still presents huge problems in many an organization. Unless you are in a senior position, your opinions hardly matter within a lot of companies. That fact is increasingly proving to be a bottleneck for an organization, because good ideas are indiscriminate in their provenance. The next successful business model may well be designed by an intern, but you do need to be willing to hear them. At *The Huffington Post,* they aim for the same interaction within the company, as they have with their audience. To that end, they have appointed 'culture and innovation ambassadors' to ensure there are always conversations happening between people, in order to bring ideas and people together.

The right-minded employees
"Several times I started a business more or less from a garage, and I always enjoyed it thoroughly. I want people to feel that same joy here, because once they cease to feel it, things will veer off-course," says Maymann. He is quite right. Most people would love to be part of something innovative. If they do not, then you may have hired the wrong staff. No longer do the right education and knowledge suffice; increasingly, organizations need to seek out professionals who are capable of translating their knowledge and

skills into new observations, who are open to change and who are able to be part of guiding that change. When employees cite being able to pay their mortgage as the main motivation offered by their job, an organization will never successfully rise above mediocrity.

Oil tankers, create your own speedboat

Another way for oil tankers to rejuvenate their business is to launch an enterprising competitor of their own. This is, more or less, the strategy adopted by Telefónica with giffgaff, the telecom provider we discussed in the previous chapter. In his open and contagiously enthusiastic demeanor, CEO Mike Fairman more closely resembles the entrepreneur at the helm of a start-up than an experienced manager at a hierarchical organization. Yet he spent many years being employed by the 'mother ship' Telefónica. It is that very connection between speedboat and oil tanker which Fairman believes has been so beneficial to giffgaff. He gained a sophisticated understanding of the operating style at Telefónica, and the deliberations there. He was also able to bring several highly talented co-workers from Telefónica with him to giffgaff.

Picking up speed

Setting up a separate and competing brand sparked a fierce argument within the organization. Initially, Telefónica examined whether giffgaff could be hosted by the existing brand O2 (a UK telecom provider). It immediately became clear that the current structures within O2 would not accommodate the necessary speed which the launch of giffgaff would require. *"Practical issues were at the foundation of this set-up, as we simply had more things to do than we had time for. We were unable to find the time within O2, and they were unwilling to relinquish their best people. Soon, the serious feeling encroached upon us, that our approach would only work outside O2, though of course that meant we could not share the offices with the very market player you were aiming to attack. They were already using all sorts of systems that could not be changed at the drop of a hat, whereas we were changing things every single week,"* Fairman remembers. It is indeed impressive, the speed at which Fairman succeeded in launching giffgaff: in April 2009 they started out in a building situated in a London suburb, and by November of that very year, the company was launched. To be sure, everything revolved around speed at that stage. *"We had no time for meetings, let alone for a sit-down discussion about our culture, because there was just so much to be done. The decision-making process was absolutely rapid-fire. Not at all what I was accustomed to,"* Fairman says.

Diversity

The brand-spanking new CEO did seek to make his team as full of diversity as could be. He had already cajoled his most innovative and enterprising co-workers from Telefónica into coming with him on this bold move. Together they made up roughly one third of the staff, while another third was recruited from other telecom companies and the rest of the staff came from completely different industries. Fairman was adamant that they would never be truly innovative if they only had people from their own industry on staff.

Mistakes are allowed

The first year for giffgaff was absolutely daunting. Murphy's Law was working at full steam. In the first digital communication plan the company offered, they forgot to include an allowance for data traffic. *"We were sure we had the magic formula, but it turned out not to work like that. We had massive failures in that first year and were very busy trying to keep the mother ship at arm's length. At one point we were literally one month away from having to fold. We had missed our target by 85 percent, and Telefónica had just made this massive investment in our company. Luckily, at the eleventh hour, the first sliver of success appeared,"* recalls Fairman.

Independent

Now that giffgaff has become a jubilant success, a good balancing act has been reached between the mother company and its other British telecom provider, O2. Similar to *The Huffington Post*, giffgaff is a separate company. According to Fairman, this means that headquarter staff do not endlessly attempt to interfere with his day-to-day management of the business. Fairman and the president responsible both belong to a steering committee which reports to a number of senior Telefónica managers. It is a set-up that ensures a clearly defined division of responsibilities and prevents too much bickering about everyday topics. Which is just as well, because Fairman is only too aware of the fact that giffgaff needs the oil tanker.

Moving from a speedboat to an oil tanker

Similar to *The Huffington Post*'s Jimmy Maymann, Sudhansu Sarronwala knows how it feels to go from being an entrepreneur to being part of a large and well-established organization. Sarronwala is Executive Director of Communications & Marketing at the World Wide Fund for Nature (WWF). The headquarters of this massive organization are in the farming village of Gland, near Geneva. If you ever take a train there, make sure you board a slow one, otherwise you will whizz past the village, as I did once. The low-key image is further emphasized by amateurish signs at every crossroads, as if it were possible to get lost there. It wasan enormous change for Sarronwala. Before joining the WWF in 2009, he had been an entrepreneur in digital media licenses and distributions, and led the launch of MTV in Asian metropolitan giants including Hong Kong and Singapore. Not quite the same as a hillside village. His experience in Asia has however proven invaluable: *"Not only is the internet increasing in significance, for the WWF, the potential growth for partners and donors in Asia is massive,"* according to Sarronwala. Additionally, digital developments happen at maximum speed, in Asia, where everyone is connected to everyone else through the internet. This is fascinating to Sarronwala: *"I have always been interested by the impact of digitization on organizations and leadership, and how this differs across regions and cultures. Now, we can clearly see that difference in how data are being used. Data are everywhere, what matters is what you do with it, as an organization and as a leader."*

From need-to-know to know-it-all

Sarronwala describes the way information used to be shared as on a need-to-know basis: if you were not part of the project, you were not entitled to it. In fact, it presented a problem if you had managed to access it somehow anyway. Just like I have, Sarronwala has noticed what great difficulty managers are having in Europe and the United States, in letting go of the system of separated and secret data, and he is very apprehensive of what Asia will bring: *"I really could not say how the even more traditional cultures of India and China will deal with this. It is completely alien to them, far beyond their DNA."*

We continue to talk about the fading hierarchy. According to Sarronwala, many managers find the distance between themselves and their employees to be extremely important, as they feel it conveys part of their status. Digital applications like Yammer are shrinking this distance as we speak: *"We are really only at the beginning, now. Within organizations, things are happening very quickly, because when these new methods of communication catch on, there will be no turning back,"* Sarronwala concludes.

A new collaboration

He talks about one of the first projects where he noticed how digital technology enabled a whole new way of collaborating, hardly requiring any management or guidance from higher-up: Project Earth Hour – an annual event for as many people as possible to symbolically switch off all their lights for one hour. This global project was run by a team of eight staff members, initially operating from Sydney and now working in Singapore. It is a massive operation, where all the WWF offices in eighty countries needed to communicate with each other, and with another eighty outside partners as well. All the communication happens on Yammer. The choice for this was a crucial one, in order to run the project with such a core team. Sarronwala explains: "*There is simply no other way to gather so many people together onto a horizontal platform. Using traditional email was not a viable alternative. Yammer was the only way to take part in the project. That was where all the information was, nowhere else.*"

Transparent and efficient

Initially set up as a pilot, Yammer has been such a decided success that there are currently over twenty WWF groups using the tool. "*Suddenly, we can communicate with hundreds of people without email overload playing a part,*" Sarronwala enthuses. "*I wonder how long it will be before the use of email within organizations sees a drastic decline. Particularly when leaders set an example, employees are relatively quick at giving it up. It is then that they experience the many more efficient and transparent methods to share information and collaborate. Just the simple fact of being able to share what you are working on and proceeding to discuss it with others is revolutionary compared to the indiscriminate replies to CC emails, which only lead to a chaotic mess.*"

Taking a sip from the espresso he made himself, he continues: "*Just look at my children. They do not use email and neither do their friends, by the way. So I cannot use that as a communication tool with them. We need to change and we need to direct that change, because if I were to say 'Let's give up email', they would think I had lost my mind, but my children are actually wondering what email is anyway. I have noticed a shift in the tools I am using, myself. It is perfectly easy for me to communicate with Communication Officers outside the organization, in Europe for instance, through platforms like Twitter or LinkedIn. The conversations are stored there and easy to retrieve. For ages, you did not need to be in the same building, but now you need not even be in the same country, to still work together efficiently.*" In fact, Sarronwala cites his own team of marketing exerts as a prime example. They need to be present in the cities where 'it' is happening, like London, Geneva and Singapore. The marketing experts decide for themselves which team to operate and which tools to use; not by using the principle which the WWF dictates to them, but those tools which are most appropriate for the work or collaboration at hand.

My conversation with Sarronwala is yet another instance of large organizations being perfectly capable of making the transition and becoming far more agile and decisive in business and communication. The interesting thing for the WWF is that they have succeeded in welding together an extremely precise local fine-tuning, where people are constantly learning from each other, while still being globally connected to maximize the sharing of all the local cases and experiences. The WWF is super-global and super-local at the same time.

Leading by example

Sarronwala has already pointed out how important an example senior managers can be: *"All too often employees will think, 'What? Another tool to master, but I am already short of time to do everything!' Almost always, this will point to a lack of vision on how to communicate with one another within the organization. New digital tools need to jump into the gaps, so that staff immediately grasp why they are being introduced. In fact, they should be asking for them, themselves."*

As yet, that is a thing of the future, in most companies. *"You need to be willing to lead by example. At the same time, you need to be patient. The transition will not be accomplished overnight, for quite a bit of time there will be plenty of questions arising. How do you deal with complicated issues? Can co-workers guide each other through peer-to-peer controlling, or do you need to step in as a leader? What is the role of the manager, or will he become obsolete? How will HR respond to this? – and so on,"* Sarronwala muses.

A new state of mind

Sarronwala believes it is not so much the adopting of the right tools, but rather of the right state of mind. Scores of managers have difficulty relating to their staff in a more 'social' fashion. They worry that the horizontal communication will undermine their authority, which is often embedded in departments and silos. *"Important ideas suddenly no longer come from the board of directors – a handful of people regularly meeting in a single office – but instead are brought forward by literally anybody within the organization, regardless of their position or standing. Hundreds of ideas... not just a few."*

Naturally, this means a whole new set of requirements from the management. They no longer need to conceive everything themselves, but specifically need to be good as a filter and offer a clear vision. In the process, employees will know where new ideas are appreciated and can be a useful contribution. *"No matter how many consultants and courses you throw at them, it is the state of mind that matters, the tools are in fact secondary. We are currently dealing with something that is affecting a profound change in how we work together. You need to really want it. The next step is learning how to set this kind of change into motion and guide it accordingly."*

A culture of openness

Sarronwala shares with me how, at WWF, people work together to build a culture of openness; where everyone assumes his own responsibility so as not to dilute great plans, nor to let previous political and bureaucratic habits rear their ugly heads. Often, simple interventions prove the most effective. If a sharply-worded message passes through the organization via email, it is quickly posted on Yammer, with an added memo along these lines: *"X has posed an interesting question re. situation Y, have a look at it and share your ideas on this."* Sarronwala explains: *"Email enables people to be irresponsible. If we make this kind of behavior public, people will soon realize that it is uncool. This new setting means you can no longer vent your frustrations to others. We are all equal. In effect, this is the power of self-correction and transparency."*

The end of the silo department?

When traditionally-minded organizations wish to transform themselves into the speedboat model, the present departments like HR and marketing often come into play. Unfortunately, they are usually not catalysts, stimulating the process, but rather they firmly slam on the brakes. Understandably so, just imagine working in the PR, ICT, HR or Communications department today... The boundaries between the organization and the outside world are fading rapidly, as are those between departments themselves. The structure of hierarchy is under increasing pressure; organizations are becoming more fluid and flexible. They are morphing into holistic ecosystems, where ethereal networks of collaboration are formed on a basis of opportunities and threats at a specific moment.

That all sounds wonderful, but how can these departments adjust to it? What happens when the value added by the ICT department shifts away from integrated optimization of the company procedures, towards making flexible collaboration possible and firing up new business models? In fact, what part do press secretaries, communication professionals and PR staff have to play if anyone person within an organization can engage the outside world in conversation through social media and without asking for permission?

ICT

One of the people I discuss this with is Hendrik Blokhuis, Chief Technology Officer at Cisco, for Europe, the Middle East, Africa and Russia. *"Departments such as ICT are frequently being asked to provide a foundation for flexibility and creativity, more so every day. For many ICT professionals, this entails taking up a new approach to their work; for instance, by talking to 'the business' first in order to find out where they could be of use, instead of discussing this with the Chief Information Officer. Organizations are discovering they need to increase the amount of knowledge they share, and the speed at which they do so. The question is how to facilitate this interaction, which is by definition casual in nature. In fact, the ICT department will need to step down a notch and focus its energy on building a well-applied platform where employees are able to share their knowledge and experiences as they see best themselves."*

HR

Apart from the ICT department being in choppy waters, most HR departments are in the same boat. Virtually everywhere, they are not sufficiently involved in discussions of strategy. All too often, they have themselves to blame for being excluded. Many of these departments have long since paid too much attention to administration and control and continued to lay out new procedures, over and over. All this was motivated by an ongoing attempt at reducing risks. Any form of original thought or innovation was completely crushed in the process. In practice, a lot of HR staffers would love to be innovative, but they are often held back in their creativity and originality, by the great many structures surrounding them.

> "In the countless discussions I have had with co-workers responsible for strategic staff policy on social media, they remain convinced that it is nothing to do with them. In fact it is very much their business! We are dealing with people communicating with each other, sharing information and learning from one another. If the HR department should not care about this, which other department ought to?!"
> – ANONYMOUS SENIOR MANAGER AT AUDI

We ought to stop seeing people as potential risks, and start seeing them as the only true resource of a company. Every iota of energy should be attuned with that vision. Monika Fahlbusch, who is Salesforce's Senior Vice President for Global Employee Success and Chief Culture Officer, told me about the 'Dream Job Experience' that she dreamt up. A unique experience, that is what working for Salesforce should be. She was disinclined to sit down alone with her team and think of what this meant and how they should reach this goal, and then tell the company how it worked. This is exactly why she pitched the idea on Yammer. Instantly, the responses started pouring in, from dozens of employees, thus providing the idea with added depth. Not only did Fahlbusch end up with a wide range of great ideas, it also made her department visible and endowed it with a strategically relevant place in the organization. She believes this approach would not normally befit the traditional HR department, which tends to wait to share something until it is finished and all the details have been hammered out. Fahlbusch was pleased with the results, though: *"I think I would like to pose similar questions of customers at Salesforce, in the future, in order to actively engage them in a thought process regarding our HR policy."*

Should you find this an inspiring story and start to consider this kind of approach in your own company, do check if your HR department is 'hooked up'. Roughly 35 percent of HR staffers are actually not on LinkedIn, and a paltry 21 percent use social media tools like Yammer.[8] This may well be part of why that Audi manager sounds so desperate.

In reality, HR should be renamed 'human relationships'. The foundation of working together is made up of relationships, which are far more relevant than the idea of 'the employee as a tool or a resource'. Traditionally, HR management has built on the nineteenth and twentieth century idea of 'humans as means for production'. To be sure, we have begun to regard talent from a different point of view, over the past fifty years, yet still many of the structures of old are still intact, either openly or covertly. It is up to the HR employees themselves, to move ahead with the times. After all, their task is to ensure the skills of the staff are up to date. Now, people need to be allowed to tap into their passions and use it to grow, both as a person and in realizing the organization's goals. You need to be part of the change, otherwise you will simply be a road block for others, and talented professionals know exactly what to do with them: just shove them to the edge of the road.

Communication and PR

The department most in line to effectuate change is, in fact, the (internal) communication department. Once upon a time, these workers were in fact the 'gatekeepers', the 'filters' and the 'locks' for information. I bumped into them often and it was not always an enjoyable experience. The contact has diminished now, though. I set up practically all the interviews for this book by using online tools (sometimes email, but more often social media) to reach the relevant person. A few years ago, when I was working on my first book, I spent endless hours going back and forth with press secretaries, communication staffers and the like. With a few notable exceptions, their attitude was markedly passive and at times even abrasive. I once received this curt, one-liner email in response to my friendly request for an interview, in which I had used several references to introduce myself: *"As we are an outside communications department, we have no time for this type of request."*

Former knowledge manager at IBM, Luis Suarez is candid in admitting to me: *"If I had run this interview past the PR department, they would not have allowed it. Yet, here I am. Because I made up my own mind. When they come to read it, months from now, and remark on it, I can ask them if I said the wrong thing. In fact, I did not – thanks, I already knew that – so, thank you very much. The beauty of social tools is that you no longer require a go-between., There is an immediate interaction between the customer and the company. Together, we can show them that we are perfectly capable of acting of our own accord. You and I are engaging in conversation right now. I am the best person to tell me what I can and cannot say. Surely, they hired me as a professional, so they need to trust me to be one. There is no way I am going to tell them beforehand, that I am going to do an interview."*

Vision

I have also noticed plenty of good will, by the way. Many an ICT, HR or Communication department has to wobble about, due to a lack of vision from the top of the organization. At the American Electric Power (one of the largest energy suppliers in the US),Director of Internal Communications, William

> **"We shape our structures. Then they shape us."**
> – WINSTON CHURCHILL

Amurgis, clearly does have the required vision. He believes communication departments need to switch to a simpler definition of their role: *"We inspire, inform and involve employees. We inspire them by emphasizing our values and goals – as defined by our mission statement. This allows us to help employees appreciate how*

95

their work contributes to achieving the company results, and to a better world. What matters here is the use of smart technology and the nourishing of a mutually respectful culture."

Christian Kuhna, responsible for Future Learning & the Learning Campus at Adidas, started in the internal communications department. There, he was the creator of an internal blogging system (the Adidas Wikipedia), and guided the implementation of several internal social media tools. These initiatives did not succeed in spreading through the organization until he confronted the HR Director and convinced him that it was this very technology that would play a crucial part in realizing the ambition to be an innovative and connected organization. Kuhna remarks: *"Sometimes, you need to fight the enemy from within."* From that moment on, the company just took off.

'Wire-archy'

No longer does the new organization become involved in guiding and unilaterally deciding what to communicate and when, but it facilitates, inspires and unites talent, passion and contacts. Departments like HR and ICT and their respective positions within the organization are seeing an increased entanglement of the formal and informal. As a result of restructuring and baby-boomers reaching retirement, organizations are moving away from hierarchy towards 'wire-archy'; a holistic, interconnected organizational structure. Employees who are organized according to the principles of 'wire-archy' could not care less about hierarchy: they have their own way of wielding influence. They are accustomed to autonomy and responsibility. Currently, they may still have someone above them, but they are well aware that in ten years' time, they will make up 70 percent of the workforce, so not to worry. These are the people who seek out new business models and types of organization. That is what the next chapter deals with.

Summary

There are myriad of ways for established companies to take advantage of the value added by speedboats. Taking them over is one way to do it, creating a speedboat of their own is another. Or they can always heave the speedboat captain up on deck, with their enterprising spirit in his kit bag.

This embracing of speedboat characteristics is not always smooth sailing. In fact, everyone may have to heed a call for 'all hands on deck'. In particular, departments like HR and Marketing can suddenly find themselves rudderless, with no familiar bearings to speak of.

5. A fleet of speedboats

"We have adopted a new way of talking about ourselves. From being one large company we have effectively changed into a collection of forty separate businesses. Though you may be hard-pressed to call them real speedboats, with an average turnover of 500 million to 1 billion euros, you could refer to them as a flexible squadron, making up a powerful fleet together." These words are spoken by Frans van Houten, Philips CEO. We meet in his office at the Amsterdam headquarters, which, by the way, can be booked as a conference room when he is out of the office. Van Houten seems hardly concerned with traditional status symbols, like having his own office.

From self-righteousness to value added

We talk about the impact made by the digital era on multinationals like Philips. I ask him if he thinks the current structures of organization and leadership principles are at all viable. In reply, Van Houten tells me about the light division at Philips, and the immense change of direction brought about by digital technology there.

The lighting market had been a virtual oligopoly, which Van Houten believes led to a certain degree of self-righteousness. That was the case, until LED-technology entered the market as a new technology. *"Now, LED-products make up 30 percent of the lighting market, and this market is on its way to being com-modity moditized. If we fail to innovate, the biggest price fiend will win. Should that occur, one can always work on distribution chains by cutting back costs and outsourcing more activities, but that is nev-er more than a defensive course of action. It will not drive you into poverty, though it will hardly bring you great riches either. By defi-nition, the yields you are able to produce within an oligopoly are di-minishing, in the digital world of today,"* Van Houten says.

Based on these conditions, Philips Lighting had a small group of people start working on conceiving new applications which would bring value added to the customer. In the consumer mar-ket this resulted in the 'intelligent' lamp HUE, which connects to the internet, making it possible for you to operate it from an-ywhere in the world, with your smartphone. Van Houten con-tinues: *"Just imagine, three lamps for two hundred euros, running completely counter to the trend of products becoming more alike and cheaper to boot. Apparently, consumers are still more than willing to spend money when they perceive the right balance be-tween price, quality and value added. The HUE ticks all the boxes. This concept makes home lighting intelligent; each lamp is given an IP-address and links up with the specially provided hub, through the internet. It offers the consumer endless possibilities: adjusting the color and intensity of individual lights, controlling them re-motely, having lights blink when the phone rings, give off a signal when the stock market declines or any other 'if-then' combination you could possibly come up with."*

Big data

Van Houten is, in fact, outlining a situation where digitization is less of a threat than it is an opportunity. The previously men-tioned hub is not only helpful to the user, but to the producer as well. The anonymously gathered and combined data from all the hubs in use have the benefit of making a second business model possible. Courtesy of this big data, energy suppliers have a detailed overview of energy use: which lights are used, where in the home and at what time? This information could help the industry to better regulate the use of the grid, and provide a more made-to-measure supply. *"In the end, Philips will partly become a data company. Though we shall still have to supply the light photons, of course,"* Van Houten says with a smile. *"You need to remain focused on where your earnings model is at the end of the day. At present, we still have quite a good margin on the actual lamps, but that will evaporate once this becomes a more common product. When that happens, our proposition regarding big data for energy suppliers may well prove to be much more significant and profitable."*

If you translate the connection between products and data, you could come up with myriad other profitable ideas. For instance, Philips launched a new CT scanner in 2013, the IQ on Spectral CT. Not only does this make the usual CT scans, it further provides physicians with software to carry out a quick-scan of an enormous and, of course, anonymous database of CT-scans, in order to reach a diagnosis rapidly and possibly even decide on the most suitable course of treatment. At the launch, Van Houten said: *"We wish to be the hospital's partner. Not only do we want to supply the equipment, we also want to provide the software to ensure more efficient health care. In turn, this provides us with an improved business model. We will not be measured according to what we bring, but by the results. To be sure, the competition is by no means lying dormant, but we have worked on this development for a decade. At the very least, we are not aware of competitors getting ready to launch anything similar in the near future."*[1]

Philips aims to have digital technology bring its extra boost to the group of Consumer Lifestyle products. As an example, Van Houten mentions air purifiers for the consumer market: *"Imagine living in Beijing, where you can barely do without one of these, and you purchase one for your bedroom. The thing is, you have no idea if it is working. You can switch it on, but there is no feedback. By hooking up that same machine to your Wi-Fi connection, so that you can monitor its progress on your smartphone and see how the air quality is improving in your bedroom, or to switch it on and off, remotely, or anything else you can think of. This too is beneficial to us and the customer simultaneously. For example, we are able to notice when you are running low on air filters and send you a new set in plenty of time, if you have subscribed to that optional service."*

In the near future, Philips wants to launch at least five concepts which fuse online and offline options together. For instance, picture kitchen appliances that allow you to read recipes online, and which provide you with feedback on whether you are correctly following the recipe.

A new strategy

These are all wonderful examples, but they only came to fruition after the strategy had been adjusted. A decline in innovation, an increase in bureaucracy and tunnel vision were all leaning heavily on Philips' livelihood. *"We were really on the wrong track, Philips was a burning platform,"* Van Houten once said in an interview.[2]

I press him on what exactly he meant in saying that. *"I was convinced we had to change tack. However, that is precisely when you discover how complicated it can be to get an organization to budge. Even though Philips is a massive company, we have succeeded in making huge strides these past few years. The beckoning of a hand almost always has a more positive effect than the crack of a whip – though you do need both."*

"I can hardly wait for the next generation of toothbrushes, which will send your dentist a report on your dental condition."
– MARC BENIOFF, SALESFORCE CEO

The picture painted by Van Houten brings to mind the Knock Nevis, the largest ship ever built. Its length was a grandiose 485 meters (some 1,591 feet), it was 69 meters wide, had a depth of 25 meters and a turning circle of roughly 3.2 kilometers. It was supposed to replace a whole fleet of other ships, which in turn would produce immense savings on crew and fuel. Unfortunately, the Knock Nevis moved such an amount of water that she was unable to sail the English Channel, and maneuvering her around most harbors turned out to be impossible.

"We are actually living in hugely exciting times," Van Houten continues, "It is our mission to provide the best possible workplace for people who share our passion. If you strike up a conversation about that and if you give a team some money, they often produce great things."

In the previously quoted interview, Van Houten worded it like this: "I spent at least three months travelling the world, visiting a startling number of people: customers, business units, employees, shareholders, future co-workers. A pattern emerged, or rather a diagnosis: we lacked ambition. We were too slow and not sufficiently enterprising. Customers kept repeating: 'You could be so much more than this.' Philips was not tapping into its potential. Now, I am trying to transform Philips into a solution-driven organization, instead of one that is product-driven. There is much more value added in solutions. This is the polar opposite of saying: I have a catalogue from which I push products towards my customers. Anyone can do that. The competition is growing, everywhere you look. Even businesses that have been around for a century are becoming irrelevant, sometimes overnight. That could leave you in the same boat as Nokia. Saying that 'it won't happen that quickly', is truly a precursor of malfunctioning. There is absolutely no need to panic at the thought of competition, but you do need to ensure you are ahead of them in making improvements, all the time."

Resistance

My most pressing recollection of this conversation is the willingness of Philips, and of Van Houten individually, to drastically turn the wheel to another direction when faced with changing circumstances. It may appear perfectly natural, though in fact the resistance to change runs very deep in many organizations. A lot of businesses would do well to be inspired by the attitude of openness and willingness to learn, which the board at Philips is endowed with.

In 2013, *The Harvard Business Review* ran an article portraying the board meeting of a company that was hit hard by the rise of Napster, the online platform where users could share music. They discussed the ways in which to destroy Napster for over an hour, until one of the directors, who had been listening quietly, remarked: *"There is no law that will stop social change."* He had pinpointed exactly what was happening: the consumer had taken away the power from existing institutions and the whole industry would have to face radical change.[4]

I would venture to disagree on whether online-sharing of music constitutes social change: after all, all kinds of technology are used to connect us and our passions. However, Napster has indeed been successful in undermining the power of established institutions – there is no doubt about that. That makes it vitally important for the leaders of oil tankers to succeed in translating developments into a new course of action for the organization.

Too much innovation

It would seem impossible to have too much innovation within an organization. For example, management guru Gary Hamel, writing in *The End of Management*, says: *"Innovation is a perpetual numbers game; the more you do it, the greater the odds are of you producing serious results."* However, it can also bring your company to the brink of collapse. That is what happened to LEGO. In his brilliant book *Brick by Brick*, David Robertson describes how Godtfred Christiansen, the son of founder Ole Kirk Christiansen, switched production to plastic building blocks in the 1950s, and adopted consumer creativity as the foundation for his product. That became the basic principle for everything LEGO did, from then on. But the company became increasingly entangled in all manner of innovation, which launched countless new lines of models of which only a handful actually took off and yielded a profit. When they were at rock bottom, Jorgen Vig Knudstorp – previously a McKinsey consultant – took over at the helm. Right away, he pinpointed what was wrong: *"They (the management team) were not collaborating, opting instead to operate from silos, and this behavior trickled down into the whole organization."*

Return to the core

It is this analysis which kicks off my conversation with Conny Kalcher, LEGO Vice President of Marketing & Consumer Experiences. A native of Denmark, Kalcher has lived in the UK for nearly 20 years and has been part of LEGO for virtually all that time. Consequently, she has seen the huge highs and the lowest lows. Her office in the London suburb of Slough is overflowing with boxes of LEGO and her business card is, quite naturally, a LEGO-miniature version of herself, with her contact details printed on it.

When I describe it, Kalcher immediately picks up on the title of this book: *"It is an ongoing struggle for us to remain a speedboat. No matter which way you look, there is no doubt about it, we had turned into an oil tanker. Some of our procedures still belong on an oil tanker, in other areas we have managed to switch to being a fleet of speedboats, cruising along together. By no means have we completely succeeded yet, as we still need to reach a much higher level of general flexibility."*

In response to my question about the transformation of their oil tanker into a fleet of speedboats, Kalcher explains how they – first things first – took steps to immensely simplify production. The LEGO brick is the very core of the company. In fact, LEGO is basically a production company, where the right brick needs to be at the right place, at the right time. Until recently, LEGO's range was an unbelievable 14,000 different bricks. This rather complicated the whole system of production and distribution. Further complications were introduced by the wealth of creative ideas brought forward by the designers, because many of the new products called for completely new bricks. The tide turned when the designers were told they had to use a minimum number of existing bricks, for their new designs. Next, all the bricks were organized into categories and the volume of production was adjusted accordingly.

"Change begins with a handful of people," Kalcher tells me. She believes it is more of an evolution than a revolution. Nowadays, the most important lesson for LEGO, as it is for any business, is how to find ways to interact directly with the consumer. In turn, that alters the structure, the way people work together, and the planning and innovation. LEGO's need to speed up production is really just the first step. The expansion into places like Asia and Brazil is rapidly gaining momentum. *"We do not have the luxury of taking twenty years to lay down our roots there, we need to do it quickly, and do it well, before someone else beats us to it. That means thinking on our feet,"* Kalcher emphasizes.

> **"Indifference is not the reason for changing provoking resistance, complexity is."**
> – BILL GATES

Managing complexity

As I leave the office with a box of LEGO for my children under each arm – the spoils of this job are sometimes quite a lot of fun – it suddenly hits me. The key is in managing complexity. The rise of digital technology is at the root of a growing transparency for the market, and this is the cause of this complexity. Transparency increasingly urges organizations to build on the strengths of their staff and their customers alike. This at a time when there is hardly a spare minute to rationalize it within your familiar structure and systems, let alone for setting it up, organizing and executing it. We will return to these difficulties in Chapter 8.

The question is when and where to be flexible, because as the situation at LEGO has made clear, it can be fatal to make absolutely everything flexible. In its founding years, LEGO was a hugely innovative business, but through the years it lost track of the basis promise to its core target consumer: it tried to be everything to everyone. When digitization kicked in, it effected radical changes to 'the world of play'. Instead of going after further innovation, LEGO needed to return to its core. The innovation lies not in the product, then, but rather in how you have organized your business.

Failure

Another business well acquainted with the need to swiftly change gears, is Telefónica. Previous chapters showed us how the telecom company has feathered its bed with the start-up giffgaff, but its own brand O2 is no stranger to speeding up innovation, either. I discussed this in London, with Shomila Malik, who has worked at Telefónica for twelve years and is currently responsible for the internal innovation lab. Malik has seen many initiatives to innovate pass by, and has guided several of them. Crowdsourcing their own employees – O2 crowd – was one of the very first.[5] *"We had hoped for disruptive ideas, but the staffers apparently had great difficulty in looking beyond their day-to-day projects,"* Malik explains. Another difficulty was that it took an immense amount of time and energy to filter through all the ideas and then further develop the promising ones.

I have experienced this myself: randomly requesting ideas from employees or customers rarely produces the desired results. Accurately wording the question is important, as is specifically selecting to whom you put the question (preferably experts in that particular field). Adding a 'game' element is often helpful, too; something which will trigger people to work together, instead of merely focusing on their own idea. Based on this knowledge, O2 set up a department particularly aimed at innovation, which proceeded to seek out new concepts. This too failed to be the way to win the race. Malik believes the team was too far removed, too distant, from the organizational core. *"They would ask us at the end of the year: 'So, what have you actually achieved?' If we had continued operating like that, we would have ceased to exist,"* Malik adds.

Necessity

In the meantime, the need for change was constantly becoming more urgent. The telecom industry is currently at such a competitive stage that organizations are no longer afforded the luxury of gradually waiting for their innovations to pan out. Incidentally, Malik does not expect the competition to come from the usual suspects: *"If a true disruptor were to appear, I would expect it to be from the likes of Google or Facebook. Those kinds of relatively new technology businesses are in fact our most significant competitors, as far as attracting talented staff is concerned."* No matter what, results were necessary and required at the snap of a finger too. Telefónica believes it has now stumbled on the right formula, after much experimentation: it is the lab Malik is in charge of. The innovation lab is made up of a twenty-headed team, aiding the organization in their tests of ideas for new innovations, swiftly carrying out market testing. Within two weeks they will produce a beta-version (of an app, for example). So it is not the lab which actively initiates projects, it always stems from the core of the company. In effect, it is a sort of 'modular start-up' within the magnitude of the company. It is a small team, endowed with a great deal of freedom to take decisions; these are two prerequisites for working quickly. Their brief continues to be as well-defined as possible: each prototype they develop is a response to three consumer problems or questions, no more.

Integration

In order to launch twelve new complete concepts a year, roughly three to five times that number of market prototypes need to be tested, so the lab is never stuck for work. Besides products and services, the lab is involved in innovating procedures within Telefónica. Malik is certain that technology can use its input to produce improved results. What the company has initiated here is an excellent first move toward awarding technology a far more prominent and integrated place within an organization. Malik is actually toying with the idea of setting up an innovation lab in the marketing department: *"Technology and innovation should be decentralized. If they are, people tend to feel a sense of ownership, instead of having the ICT department laying down the law, from a central location."*

A dream realization buffer

In this day and age, any business absolutely has to innovate, and that involves a lot of failures on the way. You will only be able to do so if you are a healthy company and are able to secure a financial buffer for these failures or 'learning experiences'. This requires you to weld, as a business, a culture of innovation – by its very nature, this is holistic, chaotic and complex – to a culture where key procedures are carried out in a highly efficient manner and according to a clear strategy.

At Philips they have these two boats sailing alongside. To this end, CEO Frans van Houten parachuted the change program called Accelerate into the company.[6] In the course of our conversation he mentions that, if you are an 'old' business, you ought to take an active approach in gathering knowledge from other industries. Furthermore, you will need to allow your staff room to dream up endless possibilities. In so-called 'digital accelerator labs' and 'hackathons' employees from many different backgrounds can produce all kinds of breakthroughs, in a sort of pressure cooker: innovations where existing products clash with digital and data. *"People need to be able to actually experience that room. You have to limit the hurdles produced by anything to do with organizing,"* Van Houten emphasizes. *"We are heavily involved in the company culture. Daring to take risks, continuing to learn, being willing to work in an agile fashion, collaborating through connecting (i.e. not in silos), quickly abandoning something which fails to see results, recruiting new skills and teaching people that it is okay to ask questions."*

In order to let the company adapt to this new culture, Van Houten built the longest marble-playing rink in the world, online, together with 3,000 co-workers. Not as a game, but as a means to experience what it was like to collaborate with several digital accelerator labs, all over the world. It was highly educational and had a contagious effect: *"Our staff is evolving rapidly. It is vital that we make all the possibilities visible to everyone. Initially, that may be slightly daunting and even feel like a threat. Once people see the world changing and what the tools are, it is important to offer them a viable perspective to work with. Posing questions like: what could we accomplish if we went in this direction? And how do we get there? What are the hurdles we need to overcome? All that will move people into action.* Not everybody *will do so immediately, but there will always be teams that do.* Their experiences and *successes will then serve as good reason for others to follow suit."*

Technology has an important part to play here. Van Houten continues: *"We are in the process of reworking the whole information system. Up until now, it has been a kind of amalgam of badly communicating systems, all of which are old and enclosed in their own little worlds. This lack of flexibility and limited resources for sharing information promptly, have cost us a huge amount of money. It was all being done by hand and in batches, whereas we dreamt of it all being available in real time, transparently and accessible to everyone and anyone who felt they needed to use it."*

At the moment, hard work is being done to make Van Houten's dream come true: a transparent and easy to approach, mostly cloud-based, ICT infrastructure, which envelops the whole value chain, from creation down to marketing. All the data domains have been organized accordingly, letting people use data-mining and apply social media with an even further improved sharing of knowledge and subsequent faster innovation as a result.

Acceleration by means of shared knowledge

I previously wrote about the internal social media platform, ConnectUs, at Philips, in my book *The Smart Organization*. In emphasizing its very importance, Van Houten believes it is conducive to the required level of transparency. As rays of sunlight work their magic in his office, he tells me about how ConnectUs – among other things – has brought about an immense increase in learning, taking the cross-pollination of people's ideas to a whole new level. Again, Van Houten is adamant about the need for managers leading by example, as he was when he mentioned the marble-playing rank, implementing the program of change and flexible use of offices. Partly because they assume an active role, does the staff note how well it works to share things; be it the successes, or the insecurities, that your work brings. *"This kind of strategy and execution may appear perfectly logical, but people apparently find their new-found independence hard to deal with. Even though traditional hierarchies tend to have their place in the 19th and 20th centuries, people still seem to base a lot of their confidence in them. Increasingly, we give rewards to teams, rather than 'structures' or 'departments,'"* Van Houten stresses. *"In a connected world, a connected organization ought to mobilize all the available knowledge within the organization. Virtually any important question will find its answer within Philips. The real challenge lies in accessing those answers as quickly as you can. Certainly, some degree of formal hierarchy is inevitable, but today the main issue is to fire up informal networks, precisely because employees are not accustomed to that, in 'old' organizations. I chat to anyone and everyone, on our online platform ConnectUs, I dish out compliments and I forward messages I believe to be important. Perhaps most importantly, I address people about their sense of responsibility and initiative. Our culture means doing what is best for the company. We need to allow employees to think for themselves. Our core value is that everyone in the company assumes ownership of it. If you succeed in doing that, as a leader – and particularly if you help to make it possible – you are a real hero."*

Responsibility

ConnectUs is but an example of how information is spread around within organizations at an increased rate and in fact becomes available to everyone in the company. The responsibility for finding the right information is in fact shifting to the employees themselves. There is a comparison with how commerce works: a move from push to pull. Staff will seek out the required information on their own and simply require the right tools to do so. This increased responsibility for employees calls for an altered structure of the organization, both for those very employees and their managers as well.

Van Houten has this to say on this topic: *"There are three types of employees. 'The prisoner', the person who understands the need for change but is trapped in old patterns. This happens for a number of reasons, but he is incapable of change, which means the situation remains the same. Then we have 'the tourist', the co-worker who spends his time at the water cooler criticizing others, but who refuses to take any action of his own. The third one is 'the player'. He rolls up his sleeves and gets to work, fixes problems and – not insignificantly – is able to take his co-workers along with him. The roles are not set in stone: you can turn a tourist into a player. Leaders need to open up discussions on this topic. Simply by asking them, 'Are you a tourist or a player?', can profoundly alter the dynamic. Instead of complaining to a third party about 'that idiot refuses to deliver', people start asking each other 'why will you not deliver?' and 'what shall we do about it?' In a large company there is always the element of making excuses and finding reasonable explanations about why the market is to blame, or another person within the company, but that is a fatal habit. If you confront your staff with a situation, most of them will care. No one leaves for the office in the morning intending to do some really bad work that day. Most people who are not performing adequately are perfectly aware of this, and are unhappy about the situation themselves. It is better, then, to discuss this with them, and find out what they need: 'we need to finish this job together, how do we fix this?' Understanding why someone is behaving like a tourist or a prisoner is vitally important. Perhaps the prisoner tried one experiment too many in the past and is reluctant to do so again, risking another failure. Perhaps he lacks the requisite skills. Perhaps his manager refuses to give him enough space to maneuver. Upon discussing these things, you create a dialogue within the company, solving the problem in the process."*

Together

The transition which Van Houten and I discussed did not come about without any mishaps. It called for desperate measures. A sizeable number of senior managers had to clear out their desks, because they failed to share the same passion. Van Houten ends our conversation on this note: *"I have learnt a lot over the past few years, including that you cannot effect change simply by referring to a crisis going on; you need to offer a positive reason as well. Philips employees had been told things were in dire straits for years, decades even, and that they needed to change. At one point, a voice rose up from within the organization: 'We desperately miss inspiration'. I listened to that voice. We applied crowdsourcing internally, to reach a new vision and a new brand. We let employees join us in sketching a valuable picture of the future. Management is not simply sending out messages. People need to adopt changes for themselves. Only then will you be able to say: 'This was a joint effort.'"*

Virtually all the interviews I conducted boil down to the same elements: leaders have a clear vision of the direction for the organization in this time of flux, and succeed in making the need for change tangible and understandable. Next, they fuse that vision with several core principles of the organizational culture. Deciding on the route towards the goal which is outlined is then greatly determined by the employees. They are provided with the required tools, information and, most importantly, bags and bags of confidence. The leaders in turn ensure both the culture and the structure are completely conducive to sharing, openness and collaboration.

> **"Transitioning organizations require a CEO, possibly on the pay roll, but always with a trusted team. People who will carefully craft the soul of the organization, protect it and nourish it, the visible backbone in the midst of turbulent times."**
> – JOHN SCULLEY, FORMER APPLE CEO

Group responsibility

A successful business removes boundaries between people, in order to allow them maximum communication. Sharing pays off and is rewarded, too. Professor Volberda has shown that group rewards contribute to the power of innovation in an organization.[7] A lot of innovation attempts crash, due to new staffers being involved in each separate phase. More innovation happens as a result of making one single team responsible for the entire duration of the project. Volberda believes people to be more inclined to give their attention to group activities than to individual ones. That makes perfect sense, if you go back in time, because then you will see that people lived and worked together in small groups since time immemorial, as this offered them a greater chance of survival. It was, is and shall be a practical and efficient decision to do this.

If you expect more than you give yourself, you are overextending your people. This is true for anything: information, time, attention, and so on. Turn things around: give and share more than you request from others. Reward them with something special, something personal. Paying attention to who someone truly is and to their passion, this turns out to be as equally rewarding as a financial incentive.

The weakest link

Silos and set positions are obstacles on the course of cultural change, which is needed for an oil tanker to morph into a fleet of speedboats, or so Van Houten argues. The strongest link is less decisive for the organization succeeding; it is in fact the weakest link that determines the whole flow. Previously, it was the strong ones within an organization who were able to reinforce their position, but in a fast-paced world, it is inevitable that the weakest link is exposed. Van Houten explains his strategy further: "*The pace of learning will determine the degree of your success. We can keep going for another five years, with Accelerate, though at some point, the qualities we are trying to include will need to become implicit. A person moves from being unconsciously incompetent, to consciously incompetent, to finally being unconsciously competent.*"

In a culture focused on learning and improving the weakest link, trust is paramount. As trust grows, within the organization, people are more inclined to bare their souls by asking for help. In an organization where staff worries about their jobs if they admit to a mistake, or something fails to work, or they are drawing a blank, the whole flow will become hampered by the fact that no one is helping these weakest links move beyond the failures.

Procter & Gamble are another company re-evaluating its organizational structure. In 2002, the organization opted to move part of the knowledge-based work into projects (i.e. have flexible workers), and a year later three thousand jobs (mainly routine knowledge positions) were outsourced to other businesses. Filippo Passerini, currently Group President for Global Business Services and CIO, restructured the remainder of the company into a flow-to-work organization. Here, professionals were grouped together in temporary teams and they are put to work in the precise spot that needed their expertise most at that point in time.[9]

> "I trust people from the get-go; they need not gain my trust at all. I give generously and expect nothing in return. I do not believe in making deals, between people. I know I will always get something back."
> – RALPH HAMERS, CEO ING[8]

Cultural shift

Companies are broken and many don't know is the title of the third report, in the series called Shift Index by consultancy firm Deloitte.[10] This report proves that the institutionalized structures of old are an obstacle for the flow of information within organizations: *"Increasingly, people are using technology to work where and when they want to. The boundaries between work and free time are rapidly becoming blurred. You may expect people to be using social media and other tools to share knowledge within organizations just as much as they do outside of work."* In reality, this is far from true: at the companies that Deloitte examined, these tools are being used less, not more. This is in spite of senior management arguing that they wish to use social tools more within their organizations.[11]

In spite of the responses showing a lack of overall strategy, or a proven business case, Deloitte researches suspect the cause to lie within the culture of the organization and leadership style. Why on earth does Microsoft spend so much effort in minute improvements of Windows, when it is actually capable of launching a new and revolutionary concept? After all, Microsoft launched the Kinect in 2010, the camera and software belonging to Xbox, which enabled gamers to operate the console with hand movements, that is, without a controller. Microsoft Research's own rationalization is this: "We believe a successful application of technology is based in a social process than it is within any mechanical or logistical one. It depends on people, their mutual relationships, communication and trust."

Open innovation

It is not all that long ago, that R&D departments were of significant strategic value to organizations, so argues Henry Williams Chesbrough, Executive Director of the Center for Open Innovation at the University of California. The cost of these departments had an enormously prohibitive effect on other companies venturing into new markets. Businesses spent more time outdoing each other with respect to their R&D departments than anything else, and tried to gain the biggest possible market share in the process. In this fashion, knowledge was gathered and stored within the organization. Now, all that has changed: a good idea can rapidly take you all over the world with limited funds, and with no need at all for a R&D department or even an organization. Chesbrough explains: *"The boundary separating an organization and its surroundings has become increasingly permeable. In effect, this allows innovation to trickle between the two much more easily."*[12]

Chesbrough cites the example of Lucent Technology. In 1996, the most prestigious innovation lab of the time, Bell Laboratories, was separated from its mother company AT&T. It continued under the new name Lucent. However, the new company was soon overtaken by businesses like Cisco, which in effect had very limited R&D activities and sought most of their innovations outside the company, through takeovers or strategical partnerships. This is an approach known as 'open innovation'.

Summary
Engaging partnerships with start-ups is one of the ways Chesbrough suggests that big companies develop more of an outreaching attitude. Operating in independent cells will surely take things to the next level. Smaller teams offer more flexibility, by focusing on tasks and results in turn, with teams made up of salaried employees, freelance staff and people from outside companies. They should aim to resemble a living organism, taking on new shapes, with its cells working together to fulfill what the life-form needs. Digital becomes the great enabler here.

A precise focus is required: the complexity belonging to the organism needs to be kept in check. Innovation may well take on a mind of its own: it is preferable to test new concepts on the market, as soon as possible. This new era shall only be successful for organizations capable of making the necessary cultural shift. The following chapter will offer an outline of the winning characteristics of that new organization.

6. Seven principles for agility in work, learning and business

An identical set of principles has kept appearing in the conversations I have had over the years, with entrepreneurs, managers and professionals. I have counted seven. They are all conducive to agility in work, learning and business. Generally speaking, these principles apply to individuals and organizations alike.

Principle 1 – Failing and picking yourself up

Google has a secret innovation department, Google X. The X refers to the number ten. What they do there is this: enlarge the challenges the company is faced with by a factor ten AND move them ten years into the future. In other words, the targets in this department more or less shoot for the moon. Astro Teller is the senior manager responsible for Google X, fittingly named Captain of Moon Shots. To him and his co-workers there is only one path that reaches innovation breakthroughs: constant failures. *"You must reward people for failing, he says. If not, they won't take risks and make breakthroughs. If you don't reward failure, people will hang on to a doomed idea for fear of the consequences. That wastes time and saps an organization's spirit."*[1]

Google beat Yahoo because it organized itself into an 'ongoing explosion of experiments' by talented individuals. Apparently they run three to five thousand experiments a year. A person using Google once a week will unknowingly be part of at least three experiments.[2] Most of them are doomed to failure, which is fine, because they are at least or, in fact, essentially very instructive.

Learning
Toy producer LEGO created a platform called LEGO Ideas, in order to swiftly test new ideas on a small scale. Anyone is allowed to make suggestions for new toy sets, and as soon as any single set has collected 10,000 votes from the community, they will start producing it. Aside from encouraging the involvement of fanatical LEGO-aficionados, the company has managed to create a failure machine, where they learn an awful lot, in a short span of time.

> "Sometimes when you innovate, you make mistakes. It is best to admit them quickly, and get on with improving your other innovations."
> – STEVE JOBS

We often think when we set out to do something that we must complete the task at whatever cost, regardless of whether it succeeds. Frequently, I come across people who are dragging a project along against their better judgment. The prospect of failure is so daunting to these people, whose energy and qualities may well be better put to use elsewhere, that they refuse to abandon the road to nowhere. Other motives also come into play, as one project manager confided in me: *"If we were to quit now, which we actually should do, we can be sure to no longer be included in the budget next year."*

Hard questions
A good way to avoid that pitfall is to regularly evaluate the progress of your ongoing projects. Is your contribution still paying off? Does the project have any real point to it? Might your passion be put to better use elsewhere? These are hard questions, yet that is precisely why you must ask them. According to Philips' Frits van Houten, you need to be willing to get mud on your hands, ask hard questions and examine the cutting edge. It is good to make mistakes, for the professional and even more so

for the leader. If he is not 'on top of things', then who is? Even with the experimental focus in place and room for mistakes, Van Houten still believes it is by no means certain that your organization will stay ahead of the competition.[4]

The CEO of car rental firm Hertz, Mark Frissora, applies the TOM principle, an acronym for *Total Open Mind*. The most important starting point is that your actions – and the possible subsequent results – are initially separate from your position in the organization. In this way, Frissora hopes to prevent people seizing up due to fear of failure. He believes that this kind of 'pride' has far too much impact on organizations, and he thinks it impedes innovation. Failure, being wrong, then becomes something of a personal loss. Frissora uses this as his maxim: "No pride allowed."[5]

> **"Success is made up of the number of experiments you can cram into 24 hours."**
> – GARY HAMEL, AUTHOR

"Why are there so many brilliant Chinese and Indian CEOs and entrepreneurs, yet no new Facebook has appeared from them?" John Sculley muses, with a twinkle in his eyes, and he leaves me no time to come up with the answer. *"It is part of the culture: failure is far less of an option than it is in the United States or Europe. In today's era you will only take the next step, if you manage to fail quickly, pick yourself up again and learn from the experience."*

Passion

AT&T Bell Labs is well known for being one of the most innovative businesses of the 20th century. The company invented the transistor and in so doing was part of the birth of the computer chip. What is their secret? Employees are encouraged to make little mistakes, in order to stimulate them in experimenting and

> **"Twitter was not started because we started a company. Twitter was started because we had a good idea, and it started out of a failed company. That can happen out of any company today."**
> – JACK DORSEY, TWITTER FOUNDER

inventing new things. Fear of being reprimanded cannot be a hurdle, ever. In fact, staffers are given so much freedom in the way they organize their own work that managers sometimes do not have even an inkling as to what some teams are actually up to. All of a sudden, seemingly out of thin air, they will then produce this brilliant find.[6]

Passionate people are not nourished by the status quo. Plenty of talented people leave organization because they experience a lack of room to try out new things, to fully exercise their passions towards the development of the organization, themselves and the people they work with. It is good thing that more companies are now realizing this. *The Huffington Post* CEO, Jim Maymann, shared these words with me: "Working here should be more than just a job, and if it is not, then you would be better off somewhere else."

Call for help

Many people perceive calling for help as another way of failing. AT&T Bell Labs looked into why some employees had more patents to their name than others did. Each and every one of these staff members turned out to regularly have lunch with someone who excelled at posing the right questions. When they were stuck during their research, they would put their problem to this person. Because they asked for help, they ended up doing a better job themselves.[7] It is, then, no coincidence that design agency IDEO strives for a company culture where asking for help is not only perfectly normal, but actually mandatory, too. *"I believe that the more complex the problem, the more help you need. And that's the kind of stuff we're getting asked to tackle, so we need to figure out how to have a culture where help is much, much more embedded,"* according to Tim Brown, CEO of IDEO.[8]

Similarly, research at Dutch research center TNO proves that staff members who share information within the compa-

> "The greatest innovation often stems from a person who is wholly confident of its success."
> – CHRISTIAN KUHNA, HEAD OF FUTURE LEARNING & CORPORATE UNIVERSITY AT ADIDAS

ny and outside it, who collaborate with others and who call for help, are in fact more innovative.[9]

Personality

Trying something out and daring to fail calls for a somewhat precocious personality. This may well sound odd, in this age of cooperating, communicating and sharing of knowledge. I have often pointed out the value of these characteristics. However, too much democracy in fine-tuning can in fact be counterproductive.

Founder and CEO of Amazon, Jeff Bezos, regards too much communication as profoundly dysfunctional.[10] According to Bezos, organizations need to be particularly aware of setting up ways for staff to communicate less with each other. He is an avowed opponent of attempts to use all manner of technological and organizational interventions to let Amazon staffers share more. He firmly believes this would only complicate things further, which would then achieve the exact opposite of the desired effect. Bezos is convinced that the solution lies in the self-reliance and inventiveness of the individual closest to the problem. To stimulate those very qualities, he introduced the 'Just do it! Award'.[11] This regular prize is given to the person who has found a solution for a fundamental problem, without asking for permission from his superior. Bezos says: *"The alternative – having people constantly asking for permission – is often far worse than the problem which needs solving."*[12]

"It is easier to ask for forgiveness, than for permission."
– GRACE HOPP, REAR ADMIRAL US NAVY

Principle 2 – A lifetime of learning: student and teacher together

Our highly complex era of 'now' requires a culture of organization which lets learning take center stage, to ensure plenty of experimenting and the boldness to fail. To become a speedboat, staff in an organization must have constant access to new knowledge, regardless of where they are. This need not happen through formal lessons or training: informal learning in the workplace is far more significant. An 'attitude of learning' is what employees need to possess: a sense of what you aim to learn, gathering feedback on things to improve, being the one to take the initiative in searching for knowledge, asking others for help and, above all, sharing your experiences with other people. Philosophy professor at the University of California, Pamela Hieronymi, has this to say on the matter: *"Education is not the transmission of information or ideas. Education is the training needed to make use of information and ideas. As information breaks loose from bookstores and libraries and floods onto computers and mobile devices, that training becomes more important, not less."*[3]

Learning through a top-down transfer of information is "like, so last century": convening once a year at a conference venue, drinking too much and struggling to stay awake the next day, to then return to work and discover you actually lack the time to put into practice what you learnt.

We shall be turning the tables on that: learning is working, and working is learning.

In this context, I specifically mean learning from each other: social learning, that is. Any organization will find information sloshing about, crashing over the proverbial deck, all it needs is to be released, so that we can collectively profit from it. Sadly not a universal reality yet. Instead you see too many departments being unaware of what others are engaged in, staffers wondering what management keeps itself occupied with, and vice versa, customer feedback not being passed along – the list is endless. By adopting social learning in an organization, you will succeed in breaking down the barriers of ignorance and distrust, and allow the organization to become more productive in the meantime. Organizations which manage to embed integrated learning find they have a far lower rate of staff turnover and will in fact realize a 26 percent increase of its output per employee.[4]

Tools

More technological tools than ever before are available, making it easier to learn from each other. Yet only a paltry 7.5 percent of organizations make actual use of online social tools.[15] *"Social learning helps groups of people share their knowledge in non-hierarchical ways and is not limited to the confines of instruction. Training courses take too long to develop and will be obsolete before they are launched. Most organizations today have a 95percent informal learning gap they are not addressing,"* says Harold Jarche, author and consultant on 'workplace transformation'.[16]

"A man's mind is stretched by a new idea or sensation, and never shrinks back to its former dimensions.
– OLIVER WENDELL HOLMES, AMERICAN LAWYER AND PHILOSOPHER OF LAW

Using social learning to enhance knowledge within your organization need not be complicated. Facebook and Twitter, for example, have a programmer exchange set-up, and app-builder, Evernote, actively encourages its employees to take a look at co-workers projects and cultivate an interest in other people's work. CEO Phil Libin had the brainwave for this when a friend of his was serving on a Trident submarine, one of the submarines which hold a nuclear missile. To reach the rank of officer on one of these ships, you are required to master the skills of all the other crew members. At Evernote, this concept provided the inspiration for the 'Evernote Officer Training'-program. The purpose is not so much to be able to actually do the other person's job, but to have everyone discover what their co-workers are doing. More sharing of knowledge is one of the results, as is an improved understanding of each other's position, better collaboration and, perhaps most significantly by far, a constant renewal of one's perspective on how things unfold. All this lowers the odds of solely routine-based work – 'This is just how we do things here' – to an absolute minimum.[17]

The Gates Vascular Institute, a medical research center and hospital in Buffalo, New York, has united two unexpected career professionals, in its ten-story futuristic glass building. The six lower floors are home to vascular surgery, which the hospital specializes in, and the top two floors are where the research center is situated. On the two floors in between, they have set up a place where the physicians and researchers can meet up and collaborate. The place is called the 'innovation hub'. There is an 'incubator', too, where all sorts of new medical applications are dreamt up and tested. The result of all this is to bring down the traditional walls between the various health care disciplines and the concentration of innovation in one single area.[18]

Every Wednesday afternoon, at two p.m. precisely, advertising firm Collective Agency has mini-TED-like talks, in which a rotating collection of staff members share their knowledge on a specific topic. The idea is not so much to 'send out' information, as it is to produce a discussion afterwards. These talks are additionally used to pitch internal projects to potential team members.[19] This collective approach, where a conscious decision has been made to bring people together physically, aids the advertising agency in its path towards more innovation.

Feedback

One of the key instruments to learn from is feedback. That is exactly the reason why Indian ICT firm HCL makes use of an internal online feedback system. Employees are very easily able to address any problems they are currently coming across. A real-time feedback system is the result, which swiftly identifies obstacles and can fix them accordingly.[20] Another feature is that any staff member can provide unsolicited feedback on his or her manager. In fact, people are strongly encouraged to do so. Not only is management expected to pay attention to such feedback, they are even required to show how they have acted upon it.[21]

Online streaming service, Netflix, echoes the importance of feedback described here. They have abandoned one-on-one evaluations of employees by their managers. Instead, employees now provide each other with informal 360-degrees-feedback, on what they should do more or less of, and what they should stop doing altogether or should begin to do. All this feedback is freely accessible to everyone.[22] Google has a high frequency of having its managers evaluated by staff members. The managers who perform best are made the center of attention and subsequently serve as coaches for other members of staff or management. The managers with the lowest feedback scores will then receive intensive coaching on their points of improvement. On average, 75 percent of them will perform far better, in their following round of feedback. The company adopts this approach for a variety of other issues too. Teams of volunteers sign on to these issues and proceed to get to work on fixing them.[23]

Just imagine what would happen if you compared the approaches of HCL, Netflix and Google to the more traditionally-applied performance review cycles, where staff members and managers sit down once a year to check off a previously determined list of performance indicators. Often, this proves to be a kind of theoretical exercise, because of the utter lack of connecting action and feedback. This presents many employees with great difficulties if they try to learn 'on the spot'. No connection is made between an action taken by the staff member and the – possibly, or not, constructive – criticism offered, which leaves no instrument for the member of staff to fine-tune their actions, nor to learn from them accordingly.

Confluence

The power of constantly growing networks presents a threat to many organizations. However, they could in fact use them to their own advantage, by tapping into them as a source of innovation. In *Where Good Ideas Come From: The Natural History of Innovation*, author Steven Johnson refers to the ascent of cities and the attendant exponential quickening of human society.[24] According to Johnson, prior to urbanization, there was little or no cohesion between people, at least not outside the immediate tribe a person belonged to. Due to the close-knit network produced by a large number of people convening in a relatively small area, the pace and level at which ideas can circulate keeps growing. In 18th-century London, coffee houses had an important role in innovation (in 1739, there were a staggering 551 coffee houses in a population of 700,000 souls).[25] Frequented often, courtesy of the beverage being immensely popular, and producing a gathering of all sorts of creative minds, who would otherwise not have encountered each other?

Principle 3 – Personal contact

At virtually every single presentation I give, an audience member will pipe up and mention this topic: *"But Menno, what effect will this digital era have on personal contact? We might end up only talking to each other online, or worse yet, only talking to robots."* An understandable concern shared by many people. Technological developments are moving rapidly, that is unavoidable, but we can control how we use that technology and how we protect ourselves from such a daunting and frightening outline of the future. We should not use technology in those instances and places where personal contact is possible, necessary and important. That is, however, what is happening in many organizations. The new way of working is often translated into working from home, one or more days of the week. This often provokes a reaction similar to the one I just described. Co-workers lose track of what the other person is doing, creativity starts to lag behind and people feel lonely instead of feeling connected.

> **"In an age of advanced technology, inefficiency is a sin against the Holy Ghost."**
> – ALDOUS HUXLEY

Facilitating properly

At the same time, much of what we spend time doing at the office is not, in fact, directly producing the effect we were hired for: meetings, reports, and the like. New technology can facilitate dealing with those matters better or more speedily. I was recently told by someone that their management team had opted to use WhatsApp and Google Hangout for the practical issues of their work, as it proved to be much more expedient. The time saved in doing this, was subsequently put to use, by convening at a different time, to spend several hours in deep conversation of strategy issues. By dealing with the urgent and practical matters before, there was more time and attention for these non-urgent but supremely important topics, which had previously often been dropped from the schedule, because of time constraints.

At AT&T they were strong believers of bringing talented together physically. Intentionally, they would place experts from all different backgrounds together. When new buildings were built, the design paid particular attention to making sure employees would be able to meet each other. For instance, the hallways were so long that you were bound to bump into a co-worker and have a brief and pleasant exchange of ideas. The factories where the final products were manufactured had small satellites of the R&D department, so that researchers could be in direct contact with the factory workers.[26]

Steve Jobs had a clear vision on this, too: *"The system is that there is no system. That doesn't mean we don't have process. Apple is a much disciplined company, and we have great processes. But that's not what it's about. Process makes you more efficient. But innovation comes from people meeting up in the hallways or calling each other at 10:30 at night with a new idea, or because they realized something that shoots holes in how we've been thinking about a problem. It's ad hoc meetings of six people called by someone who thinks he has figured out the coolest new thing ever and who wants to know what other people think of his idea."[27]*

Let's go outside

LEGO made an attempt to boost its innovation by hiring some additional design talent. You should be aware that the head office is situated in the village of Billund in the middle of nowhere in Denmark, at least three hours' drive from any kind of metropolitan stimuli. This is something of an impediment to attracting talent. So they decided to set up outside 'design hubs' in places like Milan. This would allow the company to tap into creative talent that is fond of choosing that kind of global metropolis as its base. They managed to forget to have these teams in regular contact with the co-workers in Billund. As a result, there were scores of new ideas and designs, of which but a handful ended up actually being launched onto the market. All too soon, the product developers at LEGO headquarters adopted a sense of disgust towards those hip designer types far away, who they felt completely lacked any understanding of what LEGO stood for. That this is not too far from the truth is evident from the following words uttered by one of those 'hip designer types' himself: *"LEGO thought it was cool that we could draw well. But no one ever told us that for the company to make money, you have to be able to build it in LEGO."*[28]

LEGO CEO at the time, Poul Plougmann and his team were spot on when they decided to bring global creative talent to the company to increase the power of innovation, but they neglected to properly join it to the basic principles and goals of the company. In the end, there was not enough synergy, the cost became unbearably high, the new innovations did not succeed in producing sufficient results and the relationships within the company took a blow. Another designer remembers: "We didn't have the proper feedback loops to get that reality check as we went along."[29]

Do what the company Automattic does. Every week, they gather staff members together and have them give short presentations (along the lines of TED Talks) to one another. Give them freedom as to format and content, the only rule is that they have to be about a person's passion. Record the presentation and stream it live through the internet, to allow co-workers who are out of the office, or working in other locations, be they in the same country or anywhere in the world, to see it too. Get them involved too, by letting them participate on Twitter or Google Hangout. Afterwards, put the streams onto YouTube or the intranet for staff who want to view them at a later time. Finish each session off with an equally brief brainstorm session (ten minutes or so), to see what people take from the presentation, and where it is possible to translate this into improvements to the organization, and products and/or services. Should it not be an option, translating that is, never mind. The main thing is to reinforce personal contact, share each other's passion and take a look outside the proverbial box.

Frequent contact

Scientific research offers some support for having staff physically work together, if you aim to stimulate innovation. One example of this is Isaac Kohane's research into the connection between physical distance and the quality of collaboration.[30] Kohane succeeded in showing that the quality of scientific publications

> **"You ought never to do something important without having met the relevant person in real life."**
> – KAI HATTENDORF, RESPONSIBLE FOR DIGITAL BUSINESS, COMMUNICATION& MARKETING AT MESSE FRANKFURT

increased proportionally depending on how close the joint authors lived to each other, as measured according to frequency of citations by other academics. Similarly, researcher Stefan Hennemann and his colleagues proved that local collaboration between scientists is between ten and fifty times more likely, than having a similar collaboration happen on an international basis. This is true despite all the technology available to bridge geographical distance.[31]

Being in very frequent contact with co-workers is one of the most important ways to get ample feedback on your own activities. In principle, you could reach this by using technological tools. In fact, LEGO could have used digital aids in order to bridge the physical gap between the various locations. However, even this proved beyond the reach of LEGO management. *"To be frank, there weren't any software experts in top management,"* one of the designers confesses...[32] The limited nature of ICT knowledge in management resulted in insufficient use of digital tools to increase mutual contact and enhance and speed up the flow of feedback. Not only did management cut the creative staff off from feedback, but they implicated themselves too.

Chance encounters

In his biography of Steve Jobs, Walter Isaacson provides a description of a time when Jobs was on the board of Pixar, the animation studio. Plans for a newly built office included separate buildings for the various departments at Pixar. However, Jobs literally swept these plans from the table upon seeing them. Encounters and collaboration were to be key. This led to a design being produced with a massive atrium, which all the offices opened into, encouraging the staff, or even forcing them to meet each other. This is how Jobs envisaged it: *"If a building doesn't encourage collaboration, you'll lose a lot of innovation and the magic that's sparked by serendipity."*[33] Throughout his career, Jobs engaged in the undermining of set positions and breaking down walls between departments, often without employees realizing what he was up to.

Innovative space

Are you feeling in the mood – inspired by Steve Jobs, perchance? – to remodel your offices tomorrow? Make sure the spaces are as high as can be. At the University of Minnesota, Joan Meyers-Levy discovered that people who work in high-ceilinged offices are more inclined to conceive of unexpected pairings, which form the genesis of innovation.[35] Besides, do the bare minimum of cleaning up your desk, because the messier the desk, the more creative you will be.[36] Speaking of which, the man responsible for anything regarding learning at Adidas, Tony Kuhna, told me how staffers designed the furniture for their training locations in conjunction with IKEA. This not only resulted in furniture being in perfect synch with their needs, it also provided another example of learning through offering outside professionals a peek into the organization.

Principle 4 – Bringing speed and savvy to work and learning

This digital age is continuing to chip away at the reaction time to any given action. To stay relevant in this era of today, your knowledge needs to be evermore up to date. All the knowledge you accrued in your degree or management development program, has lost a great deal of its value, and having faith in prior sources of information is no longer adequate, either. Why should you spend eight weeks waiting for the latest issue of your trade publication, or for someone to update the magazine's website, when you can read your industry's relevant news on your Twitter feed. A piece of cake to set up, yet a paltry 10 percent of professionals make use of Twitter as a tool to keep up.[38]

Go to virtual conferences. Being there in person is often expensive, involves travel and besides, most of what you hear there, will make no lasting impression because only a few of the seminars will be of actual interest to you. A conference is easy to follow online. On Twitter you can – for instance – read posts with the specifically chosen hashtag (#), for contributions, summaries and responses from the audience. Speakers are frequently more than willing to answer a few questions on Twitter, too. Add to that the fact that presentations are being streamed live, more often than not, or at the very least made available online that very day, if not within a few hours. If networking is your main motivation to attend the conference, simply show up at the (free) drinks afterwards.

Alternatives to email

On an average working day, many people feel a staggering amount of time slipping away, spent on tasks that are in fact not productive in the sense of the work they were hired to do. Freelance change expert and former IBM consultant, Luis Suarez, is one of the growing crowd of people who try to severely limit the use of email, or preferably eliminate it altogether. Luis believes we are addicted to email, even though it very much remains to be seen if the bulk of what we send each other is absolutely essential information. His tip is to simply stop replying to email, even just for a day (though a week would be better yet). This does not mean not responding altogether, simply doing it live, or through an alternative medium. You will be forced to experiment with other tools. Luis himself discovered an 80 percent drop in the number of emails, without his work being affected in any way: "*Often, email is an excuse to not meet up with someone; people who are in the same building, persist in constantly sending each other emails. You simply cannot image how much work this produces, which is barely – if at all – relevant to your actual job. Minimizing the use of email has made a spectacular difference to how productive I am.*"

> Unsubscribe from all your online newsletters. You will be amazed at how much less email you receive in the process. You will most likely have forgotten ever signing up, or have realized after reading one of them, that it has little news value to you. Your first instinct will probably be to simply delete newsletters as they appear. However, in the long run, it is far more efficient to take those extra steps in order to unsubscribe. If any of the senders prove relentless, simply block them from your email inbox.

In *The Present Shock,* Douglas Rushkoff describes the impact of email: "*Looked at in terms of flowing and static information, the email inbox is one, big, unfinishable loop.*" Even though we have consciously opened ourselves up to being email recipients, Rushkoff believes we have no control over what comes crashing down on us, whenever we open a specific email message: "*The problem is that the sender may have spring-loaded a whole lot of time and energy into that message, so that clicking on it is like opening a Pandora's box of data and responsibilities. A week of the sender's preparation can instantaneously fold into our present.*"

When organizations succeed in making their internal communication more holistic, one of the related benefits is that the speed at which knowledge is shared will increase accordingly. Questions being answered promptly is a great catalyst to increased productivity, as research has repeatedly shown.[39] Whenever leaders respond to messages quickly, their contacts will follow suit. Not only does this lead to an increased swiftness in decision-making, it additionally diminishes the number of overlapping topics that involve decisions in the first place. To put it simply: in-trays will overflow less.

Research also proves that the sense of information overload does not stem from the many emails, tweets and so on, as it does from the need to dig for relevant information. Brief and concise messages are better at inciting responses from people than long-winded and verbose ones are.

Here too, then, it is all about the balancing act, because anyone who persists in instantly responding to every single message does so at their own peril: precious attention is wasted by constantly being shattered into a thousand tiny pieces. Tim Ferris makes a suggestion in his book *The 4-Hour Workweek* to divide work into batches; concentrated blocks of time in which you blast your attention and focus on one specific activity.

The proper example

The management team at London energy company International Power certainly adopted Rushkoff's words of advice, when they focused on email in particular, in their aim to increase the efficiency at the organization. A survey had shown that the massive amount of internal email might well have been the most significant problem. Initially, the management team was certain of the email habits of their staff being to blame, until they discovered their own average of 56 sent messages a day was quite a serious chunk of superfluous information. Preferable to installing a sophisticated system of management, they opted to address the email habits. All sorts of things which impeded productivity were reviewed, including confusing, unnecessary and ineffective messages, which often provoked equally pointless responses. For themselves they set a target of reducing emails by 20 percent, and in fact succeeded. After some training in how to communicate effectively including weekly feedback, they saw a 54 percent reduction. This effect had a trickle-down effect on other staff members, who. with no training whatsoever incidentally, were able to cut back their emails by 64 percent. This all ended up saving the company in excess of 10,000 working hours and a 7 percent increase in productivity.[40]

> Several times a year, organize a so-called 'hack day'. Spend a full day together tackling a challenge which the business is facing, that's the idea. It could have you jointly designing a new service, setting up a cost-reduction plan, or improving the production line. Anyone who is not essential to the running of the company can join in. If possible, invite people from outside the organization, such as customers, suppliers or even family members of the employees. Pick a challenge, divide everyone into groups and have each group give a presentation of their solution for it. At the end of the day, summarize the ideas and make sure you end up with roughly three plans to actually be executed, with a designated individual responsible for each of them. On the next hack day, revisit these plans. Celebrate your wins, for example, by, once a year, spending 10 percent of the income generated by a hack on something wacky or fun.

Internal social networks

I gave extensive descriptions of LeasePlan, Atos and Philips in my previous book *The Smart Organization* (currently only available in Dutch, *De Slimme Organisatie*), as examples of organizations which are trying reduce the use of email and replace it by an internal social network – where staffers can communicate more efficiently and more transparently. Chief Innovation, Marketing and Strategy Officer at Philips Consumer Lifestyle, Antonio Hidalgo, maintains that their internal social network, called ConnectUs, enables people throughout the whole organization to engage and participate in conversation. Another helpful thing in this respect is to be exceptionally honest in offering feedback. This applies not only to employees, but alsoto management. Hidalgo says it is not uncommon for staff members to ask questions of (CEO) Frans van Houten. Other employees are then able to offer their own feedback, based on their particular responsibilities. As a result, Philips has organized collective knowledge which transcends boundaries between departments and levels of hierarchy.

Principle 5 – Transparency

I made a visit to the CERN research center, in Geneva, renowned for the particle accelerator which continually attempts to find the tiniest possible particles of any matter. Though you might have expected otherwise, this institute does not have a closed-off intranet. Consequently, anyone is able to browse the current projects online. A number of issues are classified, but over 90 percent of CERN's data is freely open to be searched.[41] This openness and transparency are in fact the core principles at CERN.[42] They aim to be a public organization, placed in the very center of society.

Mutual learning

Of course, this mentality has its positive effects on an organization's power of innovation. Leaders and staff alike are able to utilize the transparency within organizations to improve their own performance. Earlier this chapter, we discussed how HCL uses their internal system of feedback, which is in fact a method to have its 10,000 staff members evaluate their managers. Vineet Nayar, CEO at the time, succeeded in overcoming the initial resistance among his managers by being the first to go through a cycle of feedback and publish the results online. Setting the right example turned out to be inspiring. This level of transparency ensures that the managers who have been evaluated, will subsequently look for other managers who are performing well in those fields where they need to improve. This means they can then coach each other. Nayar believes this is how a culture of vulnerability is starting to unfold, in which employees are bold enough to face their own developmental needs and become capable of asking for help.[43] In practice, HCL does not only use this tool for performance reviews. They actually use it as an instrument for learning as well.

Namasté Solar is a US company specializing in solar panels, which takes being transparent to a whole new level by having the salaries publicly known. *"Ordinarily, 'salary' is a conversation topic rife with emotion and discomfort,"* says co-founder and CEO Blake Jones. *"It has an emotional impact on us all, and in the* end, employees waste a lot of time and energy on the question as to how much others earn and their own suspicion of being underpaid." Namasté Solar furthermore has important decisions made by the shareholders, which in their case means the majority of the company, as anyone who so desires is able to become a co-owner.[44]

Taking and awarding responsibility

It is not merely for single events, such as an evaluation or a request for all of the salaries, that extreme transparency offers a huge advantage, day-to-day business may well benefit from it too. London online marketing agency Bite Studio has an enormous whiteboard placed smack bang in the middle of the office. The most important tasks to be completed are written down there, every single day, week and month. Every single staff member writes his or her own part down, and nobody can leave the premises before making note of their progress on the tasks in hand. A highly effective yet simple way to have an instant overview of all the projects and activities going on within the organization.[45] I discussed the whiteboard with several members of staff. They feel it works exceptionally well. As a system, it makes work progress easy to monitor, with all the attendant time benefits that entails, but without the frustration which is so common when you have to struggle through a decision-making structure and the designation of responsibility.[46] If you are open about who has taken a decision, and who is responsible for its consequences, employees are not nearly as inclined to worry about who decided what. The only way for this to work, however, is by including accountability in this practice too.

> A new member of Thomas Edison's laboratory asked the inventor to provide him with a set of the work rules and regulations for the lab, whereupon he answered: *"Hell, there are no rules here, we are trying to accomplish something."*[47]

Even though Google may not present itself as the epitome of openness to the outside world, the search engine titan does attempt to inform everyone within the organization as adequately as can be. Employees are still encouraged to pose weekly questions to founders Larry Page and Sergey Brin, and other members of senior management.[48] Furthermore, employees are provided with the exact same financial information as the Board of Directors, and internal systems make all the results of projects, personal targets and discussions easy to find. Laszlo Bock, Senior Vice President of People Operations believes there to be no other way. For an organization to maintain that people are its most valued 'possession', you can only be completely open. It is the only way to prove you regard them as reliable adults, who are endowed with a good sense of judgement. If they are aware of the context, employees will in fact be able to apply their knowledge and skills more efficiently. No manager could possibly compete with that. So, that is why Google puts every possible tool into play, from physical brainstorm sessions, to advanced tools for online collaboration, and social media.

Bock mentioned how he was once asked for advice, by an acquaintance, on how she could increase the creativity within her organization. She planned to achieve this by installing bean bags, a coffee bar and a Ping-Pong table. However, Bock suggested she should start recording board meetings and making them available to her staff online. His acquaintance assured him this was out of the question, just as having junior staff observe at the meetings, or letting the CEO answer questions posed by employees. Bock remains adamant, though: creativity will automatically follow suit, when people feel they are being treated as adults, in an open and stimulating environment. Bean bags might be a fun extra, but they are by no means essential.[49]

Respect

Right then: transparency is important, particularly regarding openness from the management to its staff. Here is what Antonio Hidalgo, at Philips, told me on the subject: *"In a digital world, leading will test the authenticity and mental clarity of any leader. A second chance is not an option. The levels of speed and transparency of communication are so high, that we will only be successful as leaders, if we are completely authentic, and if our words and acts are in complete mutual consistency. At the same time, this offers us an opportunity to share our interests and thoughts. Myself, I am passionate about improving lives through meaningful innovation. What I term 'digital leadership' enables me to get in touch with people who share that passion, and initiate a conversation with them."*

Hidalgo uses the word 'authenticity', but when I reflected on the many conversations I had had with a wide range of people, I realized that I feel it is more about respect, regardless of position. That is, to my mind, the most fundamental skill of all. You surround it with a structure of 'layers', including authenticity, transparency, humility and true interest in other people's opinions and points of view. As a professional and a leader alike, you will have to show an increased willingness to share, and to encourage others to do the same.

Principle 6 – The right balance

In the Netherlands, a quarter of all employees set off for work tired, and 92 percent cite a satisfactory work-life-balance as their number one priority.[50] For CEO Chris Heutink of Randstad International, this research makes clear that investing in a healthy living and a good balance between work and play, will ultimately pay off for both employers as employees. *"Physical and mental health both matter, here. People who are comfortable with themselves and have the opportunity to discuss their future with a job coach, every so often, are happier at work and – more importantly – less inclined to switch jobs. Making policy specifically geared to this will be beneficial in the long run to employers."*

However, masses of people find it hugely challenging to find a good work-life-balance. Organizations have picked up on this and are increasingly attempting to support professionals in their quest for that very balance. BMW CEO, Norbert Reithofer, has said that employees are entitled to say 'they cannot be reached'; corporate bank Goldman Sachs encourages junior staffers to actually take their weekends off, and Volkswagen has been known to shut down email for some of its employees, 30 minutes before their shift ends.[51]

Of course, finding some sort of balance can be quite pleasing. However, I do not believe there is such a thing as perfect balance. For the majority of people work will likely win. It then makes more sense to integrate work and play properly, and subsequently find a balance between being active and passive, between being online and offline. This calls for a paradigm shift, for professionals and their employers, too.

Results

First of all, we need to measure results rather than attendance. As deceptively simple as this sounds, it is apparent we are still sorely lacking the ability to properly define what the desired results are for which activities. Nor is it apparently easy to digest the fact that the road to those results may be crooked, at best. Sometimes you may well achieve a lot in a single day, at other times you will find yourself struggling to produce any result at all. So you would do better to take the children for a walk, sit and read a book or go and exercise. That is often a sore point, though; working from home and popping out for some errands, often leaves professionals feeling guilty, while they feel no such guilt trip to themselves, their spouse or their children, upon finishing a presentation on a Sunday evening.

What matters is what you achieve, what you share and what you deliver; not the number of hours you clock behind your desk. Company culture can be a hard nut to crack, though. I once heard about an ICT company, where the professionals often log in from other locations, instead of working in the office. Despite being promised the freedom to schedule their working hours according to their own standards to reach a better balance between work and play, it turned out to result in less of a balance than before. Many of the professionals ended up working more than ever, with detrimental effects, such as burnout and disruption to relationships. Ultimately, people seemed to be working such long hours, because they saw their managers do so; they were often the last ones to log off. Implicitly, this sent the message that everyone had to be on call from morning to night.

Particularly in an age where we can forever be online, it is important to 'unplug' at times. Monika Fahlbusch, Senior Vice President of Global Employee Success and Chief Cultural Officer, firmly believes it is all about balancing work and private life without being too dogmatic about it: *"Forward-thinking businesses actively seek out the connection between work and private life. This encourages a higher level of involvement, and people need not dress up in their 'work uniform' in the mornings, and act like a completely different person to who they are at home. When you manage to share the responsibility for achieving a particular result, but can still feel freedom in how and when you reach that result, employees experience such a great degree of peace. Just bring to mind how much energy and brandishing of rule books is wasted by organizations, on matters like Twitter and Facebook. Remember, we are talking about adults here. Frequently, the main issue is that we retreat from the shared and mutual responsibility for setting clear targets together. Sometimes we have clarified the goals, but do we – managers, that is – still manage to interfere with how to achieve them, or do we not provide staff with the proper tools to make optimum use of their talent. Imagine doing so in an era where it is becoming more complicated, every single day, to say whether you are working or not; in an increasingly internationally-oriented world and where working from 9 to 5 is fast becoming the relic of another era."*

Decision time

We must, therefore, be certain to remember that the use of all this technology is merely the means to an end, not a goal in and of itself. In allowing ourselves to be rushed by everything that is possible, and attempting to swallow each and every morsel and byte of information, we are saddling ourselves with a huge burden. The not too distant future shall, after all, have us wondering if we want technology to be doing something, and no longer asking whether or not technology is capable of it, per se. Technology knows nothing of ethics. Not without reason is this one of Melvin Kranzberg's six laws of technology: *"Technology is neither good nor bad; nor is it neutral."*[52]

If we lack the vision of what we wish to achieve as organizations or individuals, with all this information and technology at our fingertips, then we will inevitably be overwhelmed by it all.[53]

Peace and quiet

When I try to work out what this means for individuals, the words of Nicholas G. Carr in *Is Google Making Us Stupid?* come to mind: *"And what the Net seems to be doing is chipping away my capacity for concentration and contemplation. My mind now expects to take in information the way the Net distributes it: in a swiftly moving stream of particles."* Carr is an advocate of us making sure we regularly put some distance between us and the fast-paced digital world, by literally and metaphorically closing ourselves off from it.

> **"We are hampered by cognitive limits. Most executives believe they can take in and make sense of more information than research suggests they actually can."**
> – RESEARCHERS RITA GUNTHER MCGRATH EN GÖKÇE SARGUT[54]

Danger?

Pete Etchells, experimental psychologist at Bristol University, finds little substance in Carr's remark, because he is convinced everything we do (yes, that includes using the internet) alters our brain. Etchells believes this to be the basis for our learning.[55] The fear voiced by Carr – that we will soon be swallowed up by a tidal wave of information – seems to have been around for centuries. In 1685, French scientist Adrien Baillet wrote: *We have reason to fear that the multitude of books which grows every day in a prodigious fashion will make the following centuries fall into a state as barbarous as that of the centuries that followed the fall of the Roman Empire."* [56] Back in the days when ICT begun to appear, we could hear similarly alarmed voices piping up, for instance Richard Saul Wurman in his 1989 – fittingly named – book *Information Anxiety,* where he provided sufficient foundation for his arguments: *"About 1,000 books are published internationally every day, and approximately 9,600 periodicals are published in the United States each year."*[57]

The admonishment given to us by Carr is, at least, welcomed by William Deresiewicz, a former Yale professor. He believes leaders need to have peace and quiet to reach any clarity of insight. The invasive extent of technology is making it harder and harder to find this peace and quiet.[58] Deresiewicz goes on to point out that we are inclined to lump excellence and leadership together. All too soon, 'being entrepreneurial' and 'many achievements' are regarded as the ultimate qualities for leadership, whereas others may well have abilities which surpass these in importance, such as being able to ruminate on challenges, or to develop different points of view by weighing the pros and cons, and then moving into action. However, this is easier said than done, in the turmoil of day-to-day life.

In fact, the way to develop more of your own ideas, rather than responding to what others have thought of, is to retreat and go deep into thought. Digital technology can then enable us to take the next step and share our brilliant insights with others, swiftly and easily. This would then provoke the likes of Carr to yet another question: does all this focus on our own network not leave us with tunnel vision? It may well make us less open to views of dissent, and consequently leave us less capable of developing our own vision.[59] In other words: an overdose of networking might in fact be an obstacle to serendipity occurring.[60] The jury still appears to be out on that one, too. Blogger and researcher Ethan Zuckerman conducted an experiment to compare and contrast the front page of *The New York Times* with the home page of the paper's website. According to Carr's way of thinking, one would expect the website to lead us down fewer original roads, than the physical paper does, but the exact opposite turned out to be true: the homepage had 315 links, whereas the front page counted a mere 23 references.[61]

Principle 7 – Surround thyself with talent

The bursting of the 'internet bubble' was the reason for my adventures as an internet entrepreneur coming to a screeching halt. In order to make lemonade out of life's lemons, I decided to allow myself a few months of freedom to consider what my next move would be. As I had gone through several personal development courses myself, I chanced upon being a trainer as an interesting new career. However, I was determined that: *'if I am to learn a new skill, I should learn from the best in the business.'* I asked around and soon discovered that – in the Netherlands at any rate – De Baak was the go-to institute, with the most talented people by far. It took me no fewer than nine meetings to convince them of my potential, but ultimately, I was hired. For virtually the whole of the next decade, I was privileged to experience what it means to work with the most talented people, bar none, in a specific field. It turned out they were better equipped, by a long shot, to be a trainer than I could ever dream of being. This experience made me decide that I would surround myself with the stars of any given field, in absolutely everything I do. Instead of trying to be reasonably proficient in a range of topics, I should focus on the few things I feel that I truly excel at. I am always attempting to improve myself in those fields, by learning more from the best. Safe in the knowledge that I can leave everything else to the best people of all the other disciplines.

Making way

Patty McCord, former Chief Talent Officer at Netflix, has a fascinating tale to tell about the power of reaching for excellence.[62] After the internet bubble burst, Netflix was forced in its early days to let 30 percent of its staff go. Suddenly, though, sales of DVD-players went through the roof and the demand for Netflix subscriptions – which meant people received the latest DVDs by mail order – followed suit. All at once, three times as much work had to be done, with substantially fewer staffers. That is when McCord had a conversation with one of the engineers, who had been the manager of three others prior to the redundancies. Currently, he was putting in extra-long hours. Trying to lift his spirits, McCord assured him that she may be able to recruit new staff in the near future, whereupon the engineer replied that he actually felt much better now and had no need for extra staff. He had noticed that he preferred working alone to being hampered by mediocre co-workers, who needed constant support, which in the end meant he had to redo some of their work, anyway. Now, Netflix takes a different approach to its staff. CEO Reed Hastings says: *"When pinpointing talent is the issue, a manager ought to wonder which employee he would fight to keep, if he announced he was leaving to work for the competition next month."*[63]

You may well think this is too 'American', but it is in fact an interesting point of view. There is after all no better way to recruit talented staff, than to have them look forward to working with equally-talented employees. Talent feels attracted to organizations which constantly strive to improve their procedures and structures, allowing everyone tap into the best version of themselves, and of others too. TNO research has made clear that this kind of culture is conducive to staff having more challenging tasks, which in turn leads them to develop further innovative habits; whereas higher salaries in fact have no such effect.[64]

Adopted as a foundational part of its HR policy, in its pursuit of excellence, by an organization like Netflix, is this maxim: 'Mediocre performance leads to a generous severance pay'. Netflix believes the demands made of professionals are changing at such a high pace, that not everyone will be able to keep up with them. Employees who no longer have the required skills are then provided with a generous severance package. Virtually all these people end up accepting this, and they part ways with Netflix on amicable terms.

Mentality

Google Chief Technology, Michele R. Weslander-Quaid, described to me how she feels companies are too slapdash in their recruitment policy. She believes it is in fact better to spend more time searching to ensure you hire the right person. When I asked how she chooses people, she answered: *"Mind set is the key, really, having your heart in the right place and wanting to contribute to something greater than yourself. If they have that, you can train them and guide them, otherwise there is no point in trying."* Weslander-Quaid believes that the idea that only the young, digital generation brings talent with it is a common misconception:

146

"I have worked with senior managers who were clueless about technology, but who were so open and inquisitive that they surrounded themselves with people who did understand it."

Patty McCord echoes that the right mentality is the determinant factor: *"Over the years we learned that if we asked people to rely on logic and common sense instead of on formal policies, most of the time we would get better results, and at lower cost."*[65] Similar to Google and Netflix, Apple too is bursting with talent. Particularly during the inspirational leadership of Steve Jobs, nothing was spared in the attempt to nourish and grow people's feeling of working alongside other exceptionally talented professionals. Jobs would organize an annual gathering of what he termed the top 100 of Apple employees. These three-day meetings were cloaked in mystery. The chosen ones were transported to a top-secret location by bus, their attendance was not to be mentioned on calendars, nor discussed with co-workers. The need to keep things classified even led to rooms being swept for hidden recording equipment. Not only did Jobs use these almost ritual gatherings to share his vision on working efficiently, with the most important influencers within the company, they also seriously benefited the cult factor of the brand and the organization. In his own words: *"If I had to recreate the company, these are the 100 people I'd bring along."*[66] Steve Jobs may well have inherited his extreme focus on talent from his father, and the way to utilize that talent: *"When you're a carpenter making a beautiful chest of drawers, you're not going to use a piece of plywood on the back, even though it faces the wall and nobody will ever see it."*[67]

Concentration

In my humble experience, the hallmark of talent is that people are exceptionally successful at focusing on what they are best at, and where they will bring the most value added. One of my favorite books, *The 80/20 principle: The Secret to Achieving More*, by Richard Koch, deals with the Pareto principle. This principle describes how 20 percent of your effort will produce 80 percent of the result. However, you must find out which 20 percent that is. The best way to do that is to eliminate more and more distractions.

Focusing on the very essence and being ruthless in eliminating all things unnecessary is what Steve Jobs excelled at. Apple designers ultimately landed on the iconic design of the iPhone, with one single key on its front, because Jobs was relentless in forcing his team to design with this idea as the foundation. By forcing the designers to base their thinking on scarcity, he succeeded in opening new doors.[68]

Summary
Personal development is key for professionals to ensure they stay relevant. Tapping into one's passion for a particular kind of work is an excellent way to do this. Employers themselves have an important part to play here: they should structure organizations specifically geared towards experiments and a culture of learning. Enabling employees to meet up with each other, not just in person, but virtually too, is of vital importance. Ongoing evaluation of how to organize procedures will be essential. At any given time, is having a weekly meeting the most efficient and stimulating course of action, or would video-conferencing provide a useful alternative? How should we harness technology to speed up how we learn from each other and the outside world? In posing questions like these, it is crucial to remember that the outside world is miles ahead of any organization in terms of savviness.

Old-school organizations, founded in an era before internet, will never allow us to stay relevant, unless we wholeheartedly embrace technology. We need professionals who understand that adopting technology is an increasingly indispensable part of their job. Coincidentally, leaders who ensure their staff is equipped with unparalleled access to tools are equally important. Nor should we forget that all the technology we use is simply a means to an end. Innovation and ongoing learning need to be the main focus. The best way to achieve this is through transparency: where there is clarity about what everyone does, where the qualities lay, the progress of various projects and what the targets are for individuals and teams alike. Only then will passion, creativity and knowledge be able to flourish.

7. Getting the best hands on deck

Kind but firm, was the voice of my boss, as he told me over the phone: *"Just do what you think you need to do. Do not let others handle things that you feel ought to change. Assume that responsibility yourself, act as though it was your own business."* I was instantly wide awake, even though I was still in my bath robe. I learnt this important lesson on responsibility, sometime in the spring of 2001. A few months of working for the renowned training institute, and I had been made responsible for the impressive new training program for entrepreneurs.

Everything about it was new, the program itself, the participants and me; I was absolutely clueless about what to do. Murphy's Law was proving itself true, once more, because everything went pear-shaped. Pretty soon, the participants began to complain endlessly. I was not particularly well aware of my own doing – hopefully time will teach me that – and I lay the blame for the failure at the desks of hired teachers and the staffers of the relevant internal departments. The rooms were too cold or too warm, the beamers did not appear at the agreed times, or had I mixed the times up when I gave the information? The meals lasted too long, there were no Post-its, the list was endless. I decided I was unable to work in this mess and sent an email outlining the situation to the directors, in which I strongly insisted upon a solution for me to bring to the participants. The very next morning, I received that call from the CEO, who addressed me in words that led to an epiphany.

Cherry-picking talent

Why on earth could professionals not manage themselves, and in fact, should they not do so? Employees at the gaming company, Valve, decide for themselves which projects they want to be involved in, based on their qualities, passions and future plans.[1] Former staffer Michael Abrash has a blog where he writes that he was initially struck with disbelief at the idea that the company was completely free of formal hierarchy.[2] How was it possible to manage a business with several hundred employees? He was not alone in this quandary. Generally speaking new members of staff need roughly six months to get accustomed to the idea that there is no one to tell them what to do, nor are there any job descriptions, promotions or performance reviews – people are evaluated by their own co-workers, and bonuses are based on the financial development of the entire company.

Survival manual

In order to help new staff members settle in, Valve has made a 'survival manual' with this subtitle, *A fearless adventure in knowing what to do when no one's there telling you what to do*[3] Here you will find gems like these: *'Hierarchy is great for maintaining predictability and repeatability. It simplifies planning and makes it easier to control a large group of people from the top down, which is why military organizations rely on it so heavily. But when you're an entertainment company that's spent the last decade going out of its way to recruit the most intelligent, innovative, talented people on Earth, telling them to sit at a desk and do what they're told obliterates 99 percent of their value. We want innovators, and that means maintaining an environment where they'll flourish.'*[4] All desks at Valve have little wheels, and that is not for the convenience of the cleaners, but to enable staff to quickly move a group together to sit down and work together.

Hiring policy

At Valve, hiring is everything. For employees, it is their greatest responsibility, bar none. They are the ones who select their new co-workers. The key question they keep in mind is whether the new hire would be capable of running the whole company. Each person who makes it through the process of selection is talented, an expert in their field. These are not people who will ever need to look for a job. According to Valve's reasoning, there is no need for a manager to correct 'hidden unemployment'. Quite the contrary, in fact, they assume that the professional will attract more work than he or she can handle. This is precisely why they focus on the development of projects which the employees themselves are after, what their passions are and which projects they would be happiest to work on. *"You were hired to constantly be looking around for the most valuable work you could be doing. At the end of a project, you may end up well outside what you thought was your core area of expertise,"* says the manual.

> **"We focus on two things in our hiring strategy. First of all, look for the best people you can find. And secondly: let them do their work. Just step aside."**
> – MATTHEW MULLENWEG, FOUNDER OF AUTOMATTIC

Autonomy

Conny Kalcher, LEGO Vice President of Marketing & Consumer Experience, has particularly noticed this desire for independence in the younger generation as they enter the company. She believes these talented youngsters to be less loyal, and more focused on their own career advancement, than they are on 'serving' the company. You could very well regard this as a threat, but it is better to see it as an opportunity. *"For a certain length of time you will have the opportunity to work with extremely passionate and talented people of exceptionally high caliber. As soon as you can, it would then be wise to give them a position of tangible responsibility. This is not a generation who are inclined to patiently stand in the wings, before they are finally allowed to join in. They actually expect less hierarchy; after all, you can now be an expert at twenty-two. As leaders, we ought to embrace this very complexity, because diversity is absolutely vital,"* says Kalcher.

Joint decisions

Valve employees are further asked to evaluate which projects will have the greatest impact and in which areas the company is flagging. A lot of people would balk at having to do this, because how should you decide? Valve is careful not to focus solely on those projects that produce results in the short term. Employees who want to change direction need to succeed in surrounding themselves with others willing to join in. This means the organization does not blindly follow every single idea, passion or personal obstacle of its employees. Besides, every decision is analyzed in minute detail, based on measured results and data. Those analyses form an important part of deciding whether or not to pursue a particular course of action. *"Although we have always tried to be highly rational about how we hire people, we've found much room for improvement in our approach over the years. We have made significant strides toward bringing more predictability, measurement, and analysis to recruiting. A process that many assume must be treated only as a 'soft' art because it has to do with humans, personalities, language, and nuance, actually has ample room for a healthy dose of science. We're not turning the whole thing over to robots just yet though,"* states the Valve manual.[5]

> **"No longer does senior management revolve around decision-making. No, instead you need to create conditions for people to organize their own value added."**
> – DON TAPSCOTT

LEGO, too, has opted for a new model of management – though it is less explicit than that of Valve: 22 staff members make a number of joint decisions. The CEO refrains from telling them what to do, but instead empowers them by creating the right context and continuously adapting it to changing circumstances.

Structured

Staff being allowed to decide what they do and who they work with on which projects does not mean Valve has no structures at all. Teams do often have a 'captain'. Not a position of hierarchy, just someone who maintains the necessary information for the project and disseminates it. These captains can oversee the full project and in doing so can serve the other team members; they do not lead, they facilitate. Structures naturally occur in the various projects, too: joint decisions are made regarding the tasks and areas of expertise. In the course of a project, these roles and tasks might well be altered, should needs be. And when staff members move onto a new project, everything starts all over again.

In fact, job descriptions, roles and tasks are often temporary and geared to what that particular situation requires, similar to the flow-to-work principle at Procter & Gamble, as discussed in Chapter 5. Valve will do anything to prevent the emergence of internal institutions based on achievement and a sense of entitlement.

The handbook is crystal clear on this: *"We believe structures of hierarchy or codified divisions of labor inevitably begin to serve their own needs rather than those of Valve's customers. The hierarchy will begin to reinforce its own structure by hiring people who fit its shape, adding people to fill subordinate support roles."*

Everybody CEO

Innovative businesses such as Valve make sure, on the one hand, that their culture is conducive to offering maximum motivation for its staff, but they also manage, on the other, to appeal to the employee's own sense of initiative and judgement. They need to be capable of acting as professionals and CEOs alike. This translates into them both possessing individual strengths and being exceptionally good team players.

Flexible work, flexible rewards

Valve further places great stead on the analysis of data and results. Because this happens in a transparent environment, many policy considerations fall by the wayside. Being transparent is also a significant part of the annual peer-to-peer review. Staffers rank their co-workers based on who has made the greatest contribution to the organization's success. Their reward is then based on their ranking position: "*Valve does not win if you're paid less than the value you create. And people who work here ultimately don't win if they get paid more than the value they create.*" Due to this method, the adjustment of salaries, both up and down, is extremely commonplace. This means that Valve tends to be extremely cooperative in meeting salary demands for newly hired staff; after all, the value actually produced by the staff member will soon become clear, and their salary adjusted accordingly.

Virtual money

IGN Entertainment, a company involved in the development of content and communities, lets staff reward co-workers with virtual money, if they feel they have gone above and beyond the call of duty. Twice a year, a proportion of the actual revenue is transformed into a jar of virtual money, to then be divided among the staff. People are allowed to give all their virtual money to one person, but sharing it between several people is fine too. There are three simple rules: you cannot reward yourself, all the virtual money must be spent and you cannot give it to the CEO either.

Greg Silva, Vice President of People and Places, told *The Harvard Business Review* that the system was born from a need to give employees a deeper involvement in the appointment of talent and singling out of exceptional achievements within the organization. The virtual money which is awarded does, in actual fact, count towards the assessments made by management regarding bonuses which are awarded in real money.[6] How much virtual money is awarded by whom and to whom remains a secret, but the final tally is made public. Silva believes this encourages employees at the bottom of the list to improve their work. They might take some pointers from the ones who are ranked highest.

In order to ensure that less visible but equally important achievements are rewarded as well, a 'shadow system' has been set up, where management can be given bonuses too. Interestingly enough, 'overlooked' staff members are noticed by co-workers more often than they are by management.

There are other examples of co-workers deciding on each other's remuneration: Zappos gives each member of staff the opportunity to use their own judgment to reward a co-worker with a 50-dollar bonus, for an exceptional piece of work.[7]

Freedom and responsibility

Netflix founder and CEO, Reed Hastings, defines his company culture as being one of 'freedom and responsibility'. He believes the company benefits from people who are innately motivated and disciplined. And Netflix rewards them accordingly, with freedom and confidence. One of his examples is that Netflix has no policy regarding staff taking time off: "*We focus on the results people produce, not on how many days they have worked.*" Hastings makes sure to take plenty of holidays himself, to set a good example. He says travel helps him to have creative ideas.[8]

People who experience the feeling of being pushed to their boundaries, in order to make the maximum and focused use of their talents, will act accordingly and feel an increasing level of confidence in their roles and positions. Provided the organization is set up in a fashion conducive to frequently meeting each other, they will share ideas, have lively discussions about them, and agree or – quite possibly more often – disagree with each other. Working together in this manner is called 'tough collaboration'; meaning that you may well need to rub each other up the wrong way, to get the best result. Ultimately, employees will then experience shared knowledge and equal-footed creation to be more effective than operating individually and having structures of hierarchy.

Networking map

The Morning Star has used this very idea as a basis for having staff write their own personal mission statement, in which someone describes what he believes he will contribute to the organization. Besides that, each member of staff signs a symbolic contract with their immediate co-workers about their mutual collaboration, expectations and points they have agreed on. From then on, everyone is personally responsible for any training he might require, and which tools and collaboration are needed. In joint sessions, teams and departments work out their targets and contributions.

The collected mission statements together make up a 'networking map' of the organization, showing clearly how the three thousand staff members are interconnected, which obstacles there may be, which knowledge hubs there are and where conflicts or mutual interests may crop up. In other words, it maps everything that is commonly left unsaid or implicitly assumed, and that often becomes a source of inefficiency, power struggles and nepotism.

Transparency

The financial results of *The Morning Star* appear every two weeks in public and detailed reports, as do progress reports on the projects which have been described previously. This allows for a ranking system of all the departments, based on the results they have achieved. Annually, the various departments present their plans. Employees can then decide to invest virtual money in them, or not, as the case may be. An internal 'beauty pageant', if you will, is what forms the foundation – in addition to the level of support from the staff for new projects – for formalized budget decisions.[9]

Google Chief Economist, Hal Varian, takes things to yet another level. He is an advocate of reversed responsibility, in which the leader is accountable to their staff. *"We firmly believe in democratic principles in our everyday lives, but somehow we keep failing to endow our organizations with democracy,"* states Varian. He is convinced that reversed responsibility will become a deciding factor

"Only when it is introduced from the very start of a company, does complete transparency have a chance at succeeding. Once an organization has acquired some history, this seriously hampers certain changes."
– CARLOS DOMINGO, FORMER CEO OF NEW BUSINESS AND INNOVATION AT TELEFÓNICA DIGITAL

and lead to shared leadership bubbling to the surface quite naturally, which we shall discuss at length in the next chapter . Varian continues: *"Having the CEO or Managing Director be the ultimate decision-maker or visionary is an idea which is past its sell-by date. I firmly believe in the idea of totally eliminating the position of CEO, the current one, that is. In the future, top leaders will focus on their ability to create openness and a learning organization. This will ensure employees create value for the clients. Whether formal leadership has a place in tomorrow's world very much remains to be seen. I think shared leadership and shared responsibility will prove to be far more significant."*

It is precisely in this era of transparency and shared responsibility that we are seeing critical thought become one of the most important skills brought into the workplace by professionals and management alike.[10] Jim Whitehurst, CEO at ICT firm Red Hat, has this to say on the matter: *"Most organizations, especially large enterprises, place a heavy emphasis on managing assets, everything from pencils and pens and laptops to machine tools. But what about managing innovation, the key value driver in a post-industrial economy? We need to enable employees to innovate better and faster than the competition, and as leaders we need to communicate better with today's workforce."*[11]

Making mistakes

Chattering nineteen to the dozen, in Washington no less, is Jason Crusan, Director of NASA's Advanced Exploration Systems Division. A magnificent scale-model of the Space Shuttle stands behind him. The library at the space organization is in fact overflowing with memorabilia, anyway. His department is responsible for the development and manufacturing of all 'deep space' projects, such as the little vehicles sent to Mars. Crusan tells me how he manages to stay afloat in such a large and inherently traditional organization of hierarchy, which NASA is: *"If I push myself to the maximum every single day, the worst thing that may happen if I make a mistake is that I am given something less fun to work on the next time."* Taking far more risks, that is what Crusan feels professionals ought to be doing. It is only through constant experiments that new paths will be made: *"I am constantly taking risks and telling my boss that I will inevitable screw up someday. By setting an example, I can then encourage my co-workers to follow suit. Me saying this, as a manager of a space center which has safety and control as key principles, may sound odd, but any procedure which is aimed at eliminating any possible mistake, will slow down the creativity we need and end up costing a huge amount of money, to boot."*

Crusan describes a 2012 incident, where a moon lander exploded during a test at Kennedy Space Center.[12] In spite of this setback, the program continued. Contrary to what you might expect, when such a significant and expensive part of a program goes up in flames, there was no internal response to hunker down with more procedures and safety checks. At NASA, they know that procedures and the subsequent drop in creativity eventually cost more than the occasional mistake. "We are moving from 'take no chances' to 'make lots of mistakes'. It sounds deceptively simple, but in fact requires a massive shift in culture. That moon lander incident saw us blow up a 500,000 dollar piece of equipment. We had known it might go wrong and immediately said to each other: 'We will learn immensely from this, and in three months' time we will be flying as usual.' In fact, we had bought spare parts six months before the event. You do not take risks for the sake of it, but to make sure you learn from them and move forward. In a nutshell, that is the feeling you want to give your staff, not that they are blowing up an expensive robot. You want them to fail at the right moment in time and not wait to the final stages of a project, and have them not dare to take any chances by that time," says Crusan.

He also shared with me that if you are ahead of the troops as far as technological developments are involved, you cannot escape some kind of cultural change. Despite the steps taken by Crusan and his team in this respect, there is still plenty of work to be done at NASA. Crusan believes the greatest change is still to come. A significant proportion of NASA's staff is over 45, only twelve percent are younger than that. In the near future, the next generation will be waiting in the wings to step in. That new talented generation will – so Crusan says – want to take an entirely different approach to organizing its work, in spite of being NASA and having a strong pull.

Provoking change

Crusan himself has been with NASA for 16 years. He is a self-described bridge between the two age groups. Having grown up in the years before internet, he was instantly intrigued when it started to appear. Crusan believes this to be an interesting time for organizations like NASA, built in the pre-internet era, which will soon find the internet generation in its workplace. *"It will certainly prove challenging, to fuse these two different generations. Staff will have to work longer before retirement and others will achieve a higher level of responsibility than ever before, at an even younger age. How do we ensure the proper transfer of knowledge, and how can we combine the substantive knowledge of the older generation with the new digital technology savvy? I was nineteen when I started at NASA, and was made to share an office with a 68-year old whose presence predated even the name NASA. I still wonder if this happened intentionally. For the both of us, it was an immensely valuable experience."*

Making an amalgam of the generations is often the smart way to achieve the transfer of knowledge. Nowadays, it has become more of a two-way street, though. Many people find the pace at which technology develops to be intimidating. Organizations ought to make much more of an effort to ensure that older staff remain in the game. Having teams with a varied age range may be a useful way to achieve this.

Democracy

Tony Hsieh, CEO at e-commerce firm Zappos, takes an idiosyncratic view of changing organizations. He believes democracy to be the perfect path. Hsieh thinks having democracy within the organization not only blurs the distinction between management and employees, it will further result in an improved distribution of power, encourage innovation and be helpful in attracting talented staff. Hsieh says, *"It is important that every single member of staff – from our call centers to our management team – be able to effectuate changes which could impact how we work together and develop, as an organization."*

Precisely for this reason, call center staff do not work to a set script; this would be too great an impediment to their providing the best possible customer service. *"We want to see employees at all levels make decisions without having to get a manager or supervisor involved. Running the organization with a lot of freedom offers our employees the time to collaborate and get work done but have fun doing it,"* according to Hsieh.[13]

Collective Agency, a Portland (USA) advertising agency operates a similar democracy to Zappos within its organization, though there is, in fact, ever so slightly more control, on a par to Netflix or Valve. There is a two-tiered system: a so-called 'council' which is elected by the staff, and 'members' of all the remaining staff. Weekly meetings provide employees with the opportunity to address issues they believe to be important, and to suggest solutions, too. Any plan which gains two-thirds of the approval votes of the council, and two-thirds of the votes of the meeting is subsequently executed.[14] These types of self-regulated and partially democratic working methods pop up in surprising places, such as the Dutch JP van de Bent Foundation. The organization provides support for people with mild, serious or multiple mental disabilities in their everyday life. With the ideas of Eckhart Wintzen as their inspiration, the organization is divided up into separate cells of 50 people. Purchasing, quality control and training programs are the shared responsibility of all the employees and are decided upon together. Because they make sure the lowest possible level within the organization is responsible for virtually all company activities, the foundation succeeds in saving 10 to 15 percent of the budget which is made available to them by the government.[15]

Netflix is another example of a business which lets its professionals use their own judgment, be it regarding holiday time or the claiming of travel expenses. They have no rules or handbook, simply a seven-word motto: 'You seek what is best for Netflix'. Much of this can be read in the PowerPoint presentation on company culture, which has currently had over 7 million views.[16] Vineet Nayar, former CEO at Indian ICT firm HCL, describes 'destroying the position and the role of CEO' as one of his foremost challenges. He is following in the metaphorical footsteps of the like-minded Hal Varian, whom we met earlier in this book. Nayar's main focus is on the reversal of power within organizations: *"What we need is a global organization – and I believe a global organization is different from an American or a European or an Indian organization. If you ask me to define this global organization, I would say a global organization is one that inverts the pyramid of the organizational structure."*[17] Nayar continues: *"This next generation is an internet generation and their key style is information-learning-collaborating. They would want more value, more innovation, and more collaboration. And they collaborate in unstructured formats, beyond our imagination and what we have seen so far."*

HCL puts employees first. Nayar even wrote a book on the subject, *Employees first, customer second*. He has narrowed down five 'sacred' principles: support, knowledge, appreciation, empowerment and transformation. For instance, the principle of empowerment is translated into employees being given the opportunity to offer their feedback once a week, on any number of issues relevant to the company. The resulting feedback is openly shared on the intranet. Nayar operates on the assumption that whenever each employee feels a vested interest in the organization, they will take personal responsibility for bringing maximum value added to the customer. They are not a mere cog in a wheel; they are the very axle it turns around.

The learning organization

His entire career, Christian Kuhna – responsible for the Adidas Future Learning & Leading Campus – has been fascinated by how people learn and how you can best support them in their endeavors. He thinks an online social area is essential: *"What we do on platforms like Facebook, LinkedIn and Twitter may well be the best example of this. Highly estimable information is shared there, at high speed, based on the mutual networks of weaker and stronger links. The more adept you become at using these platforms, the better his filtering ability will be and the more value added you can provide. Besides, the amount of knowledge you share leads to a proportional increase of the information coming back to you."*

Covert training

Kuhna believes this is the polar opposite of how many organizations train their managers. If you forget to pay attention, you may well end up using content from 1950s era books, as Kuhna continues: *"And to top it all off, we cloak the content of these training programs in secrecy, by hiding it from the rest of the organization."* He has made a radical U-turn with the Adidas training program. He gathered all the information from the various courses taken by the staff and made it universally available within the organization, in a kind of Wikipedia. This means that even an intern can find out what senior management is learning. *"It is a formidable effort, to build a learning organization from the ground up. Were it to be divided into separate silos, it simply would fail,"* Kuhna explains.

Working is learning

The technology used by Kuhna, such as the internal Wikis, is basically just a tool. What matters is to get the organization to take a different approach to learning, and to develop a facilitating role instead of a directive one. Kuhna regards this approach to be full of opportunities for HR and training departments to reinvent themselves, and put themselves on the proverbial map to boot. *"At the moment, learning is very much a top-down transfer: once a year, you all spend time at a hotel, trying to stay awake in conference rooms where the temperature is either icy cold or boiling hot. When you come back to the office, you are so swamped by email that you simply cannot find time to put what you have learnt into practice, which means you forget all about your experiences there in less than a month. Here at Adidas we want to change tack: to learn is to work, and to work is to learn."*

The strategy Kuhna is devising based on this vision will have every employee spend at least 10 percent of their working hours in training. *"To be frank, the message this sends, in other words the statement you make here, far outweighs the actual percentage it turns out to be,"* he adds passionately, before he continues: *"I talk to a great many co-workers and each of them has a different idea and opinion about learning and how to learn. They do, however, agree on one thing: staffers lack sufficient time for training. Too often, learning is not regarded a valuable investment. When people sit and watch tutorial videos at work, they are reprimanded for doing so."*

A cultural shift is crucial to becoming a learning organization. We must let go of the forcible and biased ideas about HR, says Kuhna: *"In the future, HR will purely be a facilitator. Currently, they might say: 'Right, you are a product manager, which means you need to take this course in order to be promoted to the next level.' Or if you were to say you wanted to become a designer, instead of the financial position you currently hold, the too frequent answer would be: 'That's impossible'."*

Summary

In the future, there will be limits to the directing of talent. More employees will be eligible for positions of leadership, as knowledge is increasingly distributed democratically. They will have more of a say in how to organize their own work, what the priorities are for the organization as a whole and even down to when they have time off, or how much they or their co-workers earn. A whole new dynamic will be born from how technology is used between professionals and between professionals and leaders, which in turn will lay the groundwork for new relationships. Ongoing studying will become an indispensable part of work, in order to keep up with the world of change.

8. The captain as the hidden force

Jim Whitehurst, currently CEO at Red Hat, used to receive between 500 and 600 emails a day, when he was Chief Operations Officer at Delta Airlines. He personally replied to each of them, even if it took him weeks: *"Most managers would not see this as value added for the organization, but I found it provided me with immensely valuable input and the staff were thrilled by my reaction,"* Whitehurst explains. Though he may do well to glance at the tips for reducing email use in Chapter 6, it is a beautiful specimen of 21st century leadership, in which leaders attempt to reach maximum involvement of their staff in the organization, vision and day-to-day business, and where they are open to immediate interaction.

People are not robots who you can give orders to. After all, that is not how you treat your family or spouse either; else you would soon end up by yourself. However, the ability of managers to listen to their staff is in an extremely sad state. *"The average workplace has an environment which can foster dysfunction-*

"The top of any organization is generally crowded with narcissists. They believe themselves to be solely responsible for the success, whereas change will actually only truly occur when plenty of people want it to. We need true visionaries at the top, who are in touch with the base, too."
– ANNEMARIE ROOBEEK, PROFESSOR OF STRATEGY AND TRANSFORMATION MANAGEMENT AT NYENRODE BUSINESS UNIVERSITY

al connections," states leadership expert Ken Blanchard, *"People need to be given the opportunity to connect authentically and on a personal level, with their manager and co-workers, all of which goes beyond what technology can offer."[1]*

An organization without organization

"Social networks and new technology allow knowledge workers to organize their own work, and to define their own professional development. Quite often, they no longer require an organization to do this." I wrote these words in 2011 for the back cover of my book *Everybody CEO ('Iedereen CEO',* currently only in Dutch). Even then, I could find a handful of organizations which had started to nudge this development into motion. It was really a mere handful, though, and it was often very early days. Now, we have travelled along that road a few more years and I am eager to find out how this leadership trend is taking shape; from traditional, hierarchical and centralized leadership towards a hybrid type, where professionals are the ones providing most of the substance of leadership within the organization.

My search leads me to Monika Fahlbusch, Senior Vice President of Global Employee Success at Salesforce, who tells me: *"We are coming out of a clean and controlled corporate environment. The foundation of the whole internet and social media revolution is, in part, free of leadership. Increasingly, I am finding my work cut out for me in searching for answers to how that world applies inside an organization, how we can guide people in a setting without hierarchy. How do you handle the risks which occur in an environment of free-flowing ideas, without reverting to regulations and procedures, and crushing all the ideas in the process?"* Fahlbusch believes someone can be powerful nowadays, by displaying curiosity and decisiveness, rather than the power of hierarchy.

Natural leadership

Leadership is in fact the process in which one individual succeeds in influencing a group of individuals, in order to reach a mutual goal.[2] By defining leadership as a 'process', it becomes something which is universally applicable, not merely to a

> **"Leaders need to fuel their people's energy, so that they can do their work!"**
> – ANDREW DEUTSCHER

select, chosen and peculiarly defined group. Management guru Philip Kottler believes leadership is largely about change: adapting surroundings according to your influence, in order to have others tap into the best version of themselves.

There is traditionally a distinction between leaders and followers. Until recently, this was a clearly visible and sharply defined divide. Now, however, the boundaries are becoming increasingly blurred: one minute we are leaders, the next we may be followers. Author Ben Tiggelaar used his column in the Dutch national newspaper *NRC Handelsblad* to write about some research by Professor Mark van der Vugt: *"Nature has made people into followers, who look for kindred spirits who can help us, when we are faced with tough predicaments. In that particular context, a person like that is the natural leader. We recognize his authority, based upon his value added to the group."*[3] According to Van der Vugt, this specific kind of 'natural' leadership is quite different to the kind that surfaces in a series of appointments within a formal hierarchy, though it is of course a possibility that natural leaders acquire a position of leadership in the classically-structured organization.

The classic system of hierarchy – still maintained within many organizations – will become more and more awkward and out of place. Research shows that roughly half of all employees have, at one point in their career, handed in their notice to escape working for a bad manager.[4] In this day and age, leaders ought to ask themselves: *"Why would a person want me as his leader?"* That is an attitude of service.[5] Increasingly, leaders need to transform themselves into coaches.

Hierarchy for its own sake

And yet, hierarchy does still have its uses. *"We found that it reduces conflict, facilitates coordination and ultimately improves group productivity,"* said Adam Galinsky, Professor at Columbia Business School.[7] Ultimately, though, hierarchy became something of an achievement, a position to aspire to, instead of a method for uniting ideas and energy within the organization, to strengthen them and then focus outside once more. In the end, bureaucracy and hierarchy turned into autonomous entities. *"Bureaucracies are built by and for people who busy themselves proving they are necessary, especially when they suspect they aren't. All these bosses have to keep themselves occupied, and so they constantly complicate everything,"* Ricardo Semler wrote in his book *Maverick*.

Often, the leaders with the worst performance are those who are least endowed with self-awareness. Research indicates that this is caused by the discrepancy between the broad strokes – vision and strategy, and the implementation of them.[8] This would be less of a problem, if there was sufficient feedback emanating from the organization. Consciously or not, many current leaders are inclined to shut down any kind of dissent, based on the premise that they themselves know best; after all, why else would they be at the top?

Luckily, they are countered by leaders who have got the message. Ricardo Semler is often cited as one of the first entrepreneurs to vilify the bureaucracy in his business. At the ripe old age of 21, he took over the reins at Semco from his authoritarian and hierarchically-minded father. He wanted to chart another course. *"Rules work fine for an army or a prison system. But not, I believe, for a business. And certainly not for a business that wants people to think, innovate, and act as human beings whenev-*

er possible."[9] On his very first day at work, he fired over half of the senior management and embarked on an intensive program of bringing more democracy to the company. Initially, this was something of a failure, but he persevered all the same.[10] He decided to make the company finances public knowledge, allowed staff to put their own teams together and let them have a share in the profit. This paid off.

Professionals take charge

As the previous chapter has shown us, professionals will want and will win more of a say in the management of work and cooperation. They have a vested interested in their working environment, after all. They will find less guidance coming from a small group of managers, to become themselves an immediate stakeholder and part of the organization, and in the grander scheme of a network which includes co-workers, business contacts and customers. The blurred lines between formal and informal leaders are becoming less distinct by the day.

> "There are two ways of being creative. One can sing and dance. Or one can create an environment in which singers and dancers flourish."
> – WARREN BENNIS

Relinquishing hierarchy

What is to remain of the leader? What will their role be in tomorrow's organization? The leaders belonging to today and tomorrow will need to move into the frontline. They will have to create situations where people are able to develop and innovate. In order to achieve this, leaders need to set an example, which means laying oneself bare. A leader needs to be willing to put their own head under the guillotine, never stop questioning their own contribution and thus give visibility to the fact that there are other methods of reaching a target than merely treading the tradition-

> "Leadership is about taking people's legitimate anxiety about the unknown and turn it into confidence."
> – MARCUS BUCKINGHAM

al path of hierarchy. Then you will succeed in getting people to join you, you will convince and inspire them, and take them 'on a journey' with you.

Dutch HR consultancy firm, Meurs HRM, is in the process of experimenting with how best to turn this into a reality. One of its founders, Siebren Houtman, was kind enough to share his insights with me: "*We (i.e. co-founder Matthijs Verburg and himself) were both hugely fired up by the idea of self-direction. That is why we introduced an alternative model, based on the idea that when you 'give back' their work and career to professionals, they will then assume responsibility for it all and leaders need no longer get in their way. We are trying to allow professionals their own thought process on what suits them, within the context of the company, of course, and the network we are part of; but we want them to base everything on their own personal ambitions and professionalism. We could not have imagined all the things we would encounter, when we set off on this path. We assumed there would be highs and lows, and that assumption has indeed come true. Even though we are well on our way, it is by no means ideal yet.*"

Peer-to-peer guidance

Houtman and Verburg ideally have a project management organization, where the guidance is focused on individual projects. The seventy employees are therefore all required to be capable of leading a project, and all tasks within in Meurs HRM have been defined as projects – not just the work which is done for customers, but the task such as setting up lunch, marketing and drawing up HR procedures as well.

> "The key to successful leadership today is influence, not authority."
> – KEN BLANCHARD

Peer-to-peer guidance does often succeed in producing better results.[12] Houtman, though, finds reality to be slightly more unmalleable. Some of the co-workers are having difficulty in producing initiatives of their own. Without realising it, he and Verburg end up assuming a guiding position: "*We want to have a more in-depth conversation with those co-workers, to find out what everyone's real motivation is.*"

Substantial involvement

Verburg mentions that their alternative view of leadership paves the way to a new way of doing business: *"I think we are very much involved in the substance of it all. Some people may well find this irritating, but it is in fact the very essence. Some organizations are wholly unaccustomed to this, the actual substance of the business is delegated away completely. However, we feel that is what matters most. After all, that is the core of our being: what do we substantially offer our client, what is our value added? What kind of firm are we? Which types of solution do we go for? For us, this is all a joint experience, which also produces a certain level of quality for your organization. This does not come naturally, so we very much take a hands-on approach here."*

If you are serious in your effort to facilitate self-direction, you will need to leave people room to manoeuver and try things out: *"I have no difficulty in doing so. But I do want to be sure things are in capable hands, and that someone is taking a responsible approach. Some people succeed immediately, others have a harder time. When that is the case, I become more involved. Not so much because I cannot let go, but because I care about things going well. I hope someday to not have to interfere with something when I had assumed I would need to."*

His co-founder, Houtman, has something to add: *"Of course, it is all about the shift in power. In reality, this shift happens faster than power structures can keep up with it, even in a relatively small organization such as ours. The complexity lies in the structures providing employees of an organization with confidence, and they will not relinquish that lightly."*

Tension

In the course of our conversation, Verburg is explicit in mentioning the tension which exists between, on the one hand, giving staffers plenty of room to move and involving them in as many issues as possible, and being a decisive leader on the other hand. There will be times when leaders have to be clear that, in spite of having heard what employees have to say, they are choosing an alternative. A good leader is bold in doing this, and he will assume responsibility when the situation calls for swift action.

Levels of democracy

US firm Namasté Solar is a supplier of solar energy solutions, for businesses and individuals alike. It is yet another organization which is mainly run by the staff; a solid 54 staff members, out of a total of roughly 70, co-own the business. In his highly readable book, *Culture Shock: A Handbook For 21st Century Business,* Will McInnes describes, among other things, how this kind of democratically-structured organization reaches decisions. There are several clearly discernible tiers of decision-making. The third level puts issues fundamental to the organization before a committee of rotating volunteers. For the second level, the organization has instituted peer reviews, in which an individual staffer consults with several co-workers, about a specific problem. The highest, or first, tier makes the organization into an effective meritocracy, enabling everyone to assume responsibility or take decisions, according to his or her qualities and experience. Any internal change, including adjustments to individuals' salaries, requires the approval of a joint assembly, made up of virtually all staff members.[13]

At Valve, the gaming firm we discussed earlier, they take things to another level yet, surpassing Meurs HRM and Namasté Solar. On their homepage, they explicitly advertise the fact of being a peer-to-peer run company('Boss-free since 1996'), before going on to say: *"Imagine working with super smart, super talented colleagues in a free-wheeling, innovative environment—no bosses, no middle management, no bureaucracy. Just highly motivated peers coming together to make cool stuff. It's amazing what creative people can come up with when there's nobody there telling them what to do."*[14]

Technology as an engine

For many people, Valve may well be slightly too extreme an example to follow, but it does in fact show the direction in which professionals are headed. Inevitably, leaders will need to follow suit in this motion. Management thinkers Ken Blanchard and Richard Greenleaf refer to this concept as 'servant leadership'.

It is a concept which will become increasingly relevant in the digital era. After all, the distance between leaders and followers is diminishing as a result of digital technology. Providing the right tools and creating the right culture are what leadership will revolve around, in the foreseeable future.

New leaders will utilize technology to improve and give full play to their vision, their own strength and the organization's strength. Potentially, social networks are smart, innovative and creative. In order to let them achieve true value added, a leader simply has to succeed in facilitating their staff in their professionalism, in challenging them and gathering them together. This is another instance of good examples being worth following. Leaders themselves will need to pass through a transformation. TNO research makes clear that this actually has a positive effect on employee behavior at work, and consequently on the organization's ability to innovate.[15]

Professor Volberda has determined that nowadays leaders need to be endowed with a skill combination: *"Instead of limited and superficial expertise, dynamic skills in fact require a wide and in-depth knowledge base – of technology, of the market, of products or distribution – and a range of managerial expertise, in order to achieve suitable answers."*[16]

Asking for help

When I speak with John Sculley, I ask him what he thinks of all this, which leads him to counter Volberda's statement. Sculley believes there is nothing wrong with admitting to not knowing something, as a leader: *"Nowadays, it is much more acceptable for leaders or entrepreneurs to ask for help, more than used to be the case. Previously, it was regarded as a sign of weakness, now the reverse is true. I take great pleasure in helping young leaders myself. Not because I am so much smarter than someone else is, but because of having seen many things which allow me to swiftly provide a context for what is happening. Or to quote Steve Jobs' frequent saying: 'Zoom out to zoom in.' Distance will offer you the opportunity for a better interconnection of details."*

Sculley is visibly enjoying his current position as a mentor. He never had one himself, neither when he worked at Pepsi or – later on – at Apple; nobody had a mentor or coach in those days. His career took off in the seventies and eighties. It was a time when leaders were infallible, operating from 'command & control', and employees were only given the information they strictly needed to complete their precisely specified and limited tasks. Things could scarcely be more different now: the formal organization chart will in fact tell you nothing at all about how an organization actually operates. More activities than ever are centered in projects, and many things happen virtually. Some staffers have salaried positions, others are freelance.

Sculley believes the formal hierarchy within organizations will, in part, remain. The CEO and their management team will still take care of the development, maintenance and scaling up of the business model, and they will nourish the relationships with top-tier clients and key suppliers. At the same time, Sculley thinks senior management no longer needs to excel at everything. He knows the world has become too complicated for a select group of leaders to successfully possess all the answers. This was not always the case: *"At Pepsi, we leaders had to literally be capable of doing everything. Now, each stage of an organization's development calls for different skills and, consequently, different people. As a result, there is more flexibility and people are expected to be increasingly moveable,"* Sculley concludes.

Flatter and more transparent

Finding a balance of shared production and exchange has become key, or in the words of Philips Chief Marketing Officer, Antonio Hidalgo: *"There is a flattening down of hierarchies going on, silos within organizations will start to fade, as networks pop up as a force to be reckoned with. Businesses will no longer be limited by boundaries, in their work, and thus succeed in letting the transformation of knowledge benefit them."*

Christine Lagarde, head of the International Monetary Fund, has given a description of an internal platform where the managers at IMF share their targets. Whether or not the targets were achieved can be seen by anyone. Part of their remuneration is based upon this.[17] At the Google-X innovation lab, it is crucial for managers to facilitate their professionals as best they can, because they are entirely free to switch teams or projects should they feel they are not being guided properly.[18]

Listening

A business need not be as hip as the likes of Spotify, Salesforce, Apple or Google, in order to find a new way of nourishing the talent of its employees. Any business can do this. The Dutch cookie factory, Koekjesbakkerij Veldt, has been awarded the epithet 'smartest business' in the Netherlands, due to having taken a wholly unique approach to empowering their staff.[19] I visited the town of Veenendaal to see this for myself. Seeing things is not a problem at all, because the conference room has a wall of windows, overlooking the production line. Veldt owner, Kees Pater, tells me everything: *"Before, you could see nothing of the production process, nor the workers involved, which was actually quite odd if you think about it, because without them, we would have no product to sell."*

What caused this about-turn? After some initial success, the company hit a slump. The revenue took a dive, employees grew discontented and Pater too was enjoying the business less and less. Things had to change. Coached by an outside consultant, Pater moved into a process of change together with his staff members – though he prefers the term 'staff thinkers'. Describing all manner of improvements was the challenge these staff thinkers were faced with. Pater says this was not only a huge adjustment for him, but for the staff, too: *"They have had to learn to take direction themselves, and stand up for their interests and their own opinion. In the past, I would have crushed that kind of initiative."* Instead of always reacting instantly, Pater finds the realization that listening, letting go and providing confidence, to be the most valuable,

Perfectly simple as it sounds, it took Pater and his team a full nine months of hard work, many conversations and a lot of practice, to get to this point. The results are self-evident, though: not only has revenue increased, collaboration has improved, as have employee satisfaction and the relationships with suppliers.

A question of trust

In the course of the change, staff members grew in their enthusiasm: *"No longer did staffers just come to work to pack up the cookies; they felt more and more of a shared responsibility for the business. By gradually – clunking along, in actual fact – relinquishing control, they stepped up and joined in, taking charge and thinking of solutions. Though I had initially thought letting go would end up in me having to correct far more work than before, the opposite proved to be true: I found I was experiencing less pressure and I no longer need to be so involved in little details."*

Pater is firm in his emphasis that giving confidence is not the same as letting go altogether: *"When we asked staffers for suggestions to improve, we did coach them along the way. What we often forgot to ask them was: 'What will you do next, what steps will you take, with whom are you going to discuss this?' Now, before we give the go-ahead, we go through all those issues first."*

There was a shift in leadership style in the company. Before, Pater would initially stand looking over the shoulder of every single employee, whereas now, staffers report on their own progress, based on mutually-agreed targets and prerequisites. Pater continues: *"I always assumed I was the most important person in the organization, when in actual fact the company will run smoothly even if the management were to disappear."* In his own words, Pater says he has turned the organization chart upside down: the staff are now the top of the inverted pyramid, and Pater and the managers are there to facilitate them.

Taking risks

The tale of Koekjesbakkerij Veldt may sound obvious, but many of the conversations I had in the course of researching this book soon turned to the tension about whether or not to manage a business according to traditional hierarchy. This was often a struggle for whoever I was talking with, even though the alternative was frequently the very reason for their company's success. This applies to Monika Fahlbusch, Senior Vice President of Global Employee Success at Salesforce: *"We are coming out of a clean and controlled corporate environment, however, life is now taking place in a social age; an age of networks. The foundational idea here is that this era has no leadership, or at the very least a completely different kind of leadership than we were accustomed to. In turn, that raises a myriad of questions on how this new way of working ought to function, within traditional organizations. How do you manage your staff, when the familiar way of looking at hierarchy seems to* be less suited to how staffers want to organize their work than it once was? I believe it is, quite often, all about being able to handle risks. In a world where ideas can flow freely, aided by the use of technology. After all, the concept of total control is a total illusion."

Fahlbusch suggests that it is crucial for the people who chart a company's course to set the proper example. To illustrate her point, she mentions the attitude of Marc Benioff, the CEO and founder of Salesforce: "In all that he does, Marc makes clear that he is not important. The clients and employees at Salesforce are what matters most. This attitude allows him to show that curiosity, entrepreneurial spirit and decisiveness in reaching a target for your clients are the key issues, and that those will not be achieved by leaning back in your power perch built on hierarchy."

Small beginnings

I believe that any change should have small and humble beginnings. There are often professionals in place already, who are working according to the new methods: deciding on the direction their own work should take. Similarly, there are leaders within any organization who know their role to be the facilitator as opposed to the deciding factor. Why do you not simply start with these individuals? Let them help you gather up others to join you on this path.

Steady as it goes

Michele R. Weslander-Quaid, Chief Technology Officer at Google, is adamant that the most significant role for a leader today, is to be a 'heat shield'. "Organizations in flux need people who are supremely steady, because change will always

provoke resistance, even from leaders. I have seen professionals be-
come completely overwhelmed when that happens. They were due
to receive all kinds of support, but when the storm started, those
professions of support were reneged upon, just like that. Once lead-
ers have done that, they will never regain the confidence of their
staff. Employees will soon become cynical and cease to ask the hard
questions. That, in fact, may be the greatest danger possible."

21st century leadership

One modern leader whom I am inspired by, is Giam Swiegers.
He is in charge of Deloitte Australia. *"In order to succeed in this*
digital era, you should not embrace social media so that you will be
regarded as cutting edge. Successful leaders use modern technology
to improve on their own ability to facilitate an organization," says
Swiegers.

Communicating like a young person

Swiegers believes that managers who fail to understand how
younger people communicate, will no longer find themselves
considered for positions of leadership in the future. Organizations will opt for leaders who succeed in using the most effective
way to communicate strategy, priorities and game plans. Digital
leaders, so says Swiegers, have an attitude of openness and curiosity. He continues: *"Once, I shared the link to a presentation*
I had done, on Yammer. This provoked some fierce debate with a
staff member who was in complete disagreement with my point of
view. We fought it out on Yammer. Some people may have been
surprised by this, but I would much rather have someone debate
me and I then know his views than have him go to the pub and
tell his mates."[23] LEGO is another company to echo this premise:
"Everyone in our organization must understand what it means to
be social," says Lars Silberbauer, LEGO's Director of Social Media. For that very reason, senior managers are required to do an
actual course culminating in an exam, covering both theory and
practice.[24]

The Indian firm Tata Consultancy Services (TCS) employs just under a quarter of a million staff members, seventy percent of whom are under thirty years old. These young staffers expressed the desire to use an alternative way to communicate internally. As a result, an online social network was set up, where they can share knowledge, collaborate and offer feedback. *"There is no point in baby-boomers and Generation X saying that Gen Y should behave like us. We have to behave like them,"* says Ajoy Mukherjee, Global Head and Vice President of Human Resources.[25]

Bill George, Professor of Management at Harvard Business School, feels the use of social media should be part of the job description for every single manager and leader. *"People want CEOs who are true. They want to know what you are thinking. And whether you can think of a cheaper way to reach your client base and your staff at once?"*[26]

Sailing on instruments

Not all leaders are equally successful in making this shift. In *The Velocity Manifesto: Harnessing Technology, Vision and Culture to Future-Proof your Organization*, Scott Klososky paints a picture of more conservative industries (manufacturing, banking and insurance, accountancy) finding their leaders paralyzed by the new surroundings instead of adjusting to them. Klososky notices many estimable qualities in those leaders, but they lack precisely those skills which have become so very essential today. According to Klososky they will find themselves in choppy waters in the next decade.

Bert Sandle, Director of Technical Excellence at gaming titan Electronic Arts, recently told me about their implementing an internal social network. He feels that, even though senior management often realizes the advantages of putting digital technology to use for communication and sharing knowledge, they often have great difficulty in participating themselves. This often proves disastrous in the signal it sends to the rest of the company. After all, why would you fail to use something which you profess to be important, particularly when it is a communication tool?

There are too many leaders – I see this in practice daily – who are clueless about all manner of new developments in the market; about the changes in their customers' preferences and the discussions between their employees. They sail on the instruments which are provided by the handful of staff who provide them with information. Well, that is nice and safe, because you need not admit to not knowing something, or not understanding, nor will you be required to debate with people who are of a different mind. In the meantime, any young and digitally-savvy staffer has swifter access to more – and frequently better – information than the traditionally-minded CEO, and by following a few thousand people on Twitter you soon hone the skill of quickly filtering and putting information in context.

Carlos Domingo, former CEO of New Business and Innovation at Telefónica Digital, believes we are by no means at our destination, as far as getting leaders from older generations to join in with the change: *"The use of social technology in organizations leads to resistance from leaders who are attached to a feeling of control; those who are managing by fear and intimidation, who hold onto their power and influence by clinging to information, or who believe that their degree, intellect and experience legitimize them taking any important decision on their own, without using input from others. The clash between this style of leadership, and the promise and opportunities offered by social technology, will carry us along for several more years."*

"It is all about permeability. Not only do we need to talk more openly than we did before, we also need to remove a very important barrier and that barrier is that I am right, that my way is the right way. So if you look at all the traditional societies, there is always someone speaking down unto the people, reading from a stone tablet, saying 'I know something you don't know.'"
– ELLEN LEANSE, ADVISOR, INVESTOR AND FORMER SENIOR MANAGER AT GOOGLE, FACEBOOK AND APPLE

Reinforcing positions

Domingo thinks professionals will always look to their leaders in order to decide which path to take, and that includes the use of new technology. Which is why leaders could actually use technology to reinforce their own position: *"The world is only going to grow in complexity, from now on. Changes will tumble out, one after the other, and we will see more uncertainties as a result. No longer will positions of hierarchy be self-evident, roles are becoming increasingly fluid. Leaders will need new instruments then, too, in order to retain some relevance in the new situation."*

Next, Domingo proposes that leaders would be wise to share their ideas and strategies within the organization more, in order to both enrich them and to connect to the employees more, too. Domingo believes transparent and open communication to be the most significant foundation for employee confidence. In an open and transparent world, any discrepancies between what you say and what you do are bound to surface, and pretty quickly at that. There is barely sufficient time, if any at all, to devise a communications strategy.

Insurance firm Humana makes use of online simulations to try out certain strategies or new procedures with staff members, to test them and to elicit tips and ideas for improvement from the people involved. This is based on the conviction that the organization as a whole is far better suited to come up with solutions for challenges.

In New York, Jimmy Maymann, CEO at *The Huffington Post*, tells me he finds it obvious that a leader should be available and approachable, even for – or in fact, specifically for – people from outside the organization. Maymann is convinced that if you want to have a modern profile as an organization, you need to use social technology yourself, as a leader: *"I think it is important that anyone, particularly leaders, experience and use social tools. They can benefit you enormously, if used well. I confess, it is harder for leaders to use them efficiently and, more importantly, authentically. You will be flooded by so much 'input' that you may be inclined to set up an 'answering machine', which will lead you further astray; people are cynical and smart and will see through this instantly."*

Virtual management

We have already noticed that management and collaboration both require surroundings in which people are able to meet each other based on a passion, which then inspires them to contribute to an organization and its goals. Both the culture and the structure need to be geared toward maximizing contact between people from a wide range of backgrounds and skill sets. Inflexible departments and 'sectarianism' must not interfere and should be dismantled, as much as possible. At the same time, this era of 'now', calls for organization with a smaller core staff and a flexible 'skin'. We shall have to become accustomed to working together virtually more often than not.

But what happens when you end up barely seeing the people you provide facilities for, because they are working all over the place, except in the same office together, every day. How does a leader handle an organization which is so agile that it is in fact a virtual, almost intangible unit? In the near future, there will be 1.3 billion 'mobile workers', professionals who are able to do their work anywhere they please, courtesy of digital technology.[27] For instance, at IBM practically half of the staff no longer have a fixed place to work. At Canadian telecom giant, Telus, that number has gone up to just shy of 70 percent. Ever since, employees have been able to stay virtually connected regardless of location, and can work on projects together. The company's productivity has increased by 5 percent.

In Chapter 2, I discussed the real challenges for organizations to succeed in connecting this intensely varied group of professionals to them. If they do manage to succeed, the next challenge is just around the corner. While a flexible and graceful organization may be becoming a greater strength by the minute, it is still hugely complex. A study by senior management at Oracle makes clear that leaders currently face two important obstacles in their method of collaboration: how do you efficiently connect to virtual members of your team, and how do you build a network where these virtual employees are able to work together?[28]

A person who deals with this complexity daily, heading a widely diverse and partly virtual team, is Hendrik Blokhuis,

Cisco's Chief Technology Officer for Europe, the Middle East, Africa and Russia. *"Achieving a more creative, more efficient organization is my greatest battle of all. I will not manage it by asking for one hundred extra staffers, because I am not going to get them, anyway. The key is to unleash and share all the knowledge already available to us, never mind how obvious that may sound. I frequently ask my people to not work as single, lone neurons, but to be one huge intelligent brain, whose strength lies in its connections,"* Blokhuis explains. Simply being a good engineer is not enough. For example, if you are one, then what matters is how you can best pass your knowledge on to others, and how you could learn from them as well. *"That produces a new kind of leadership. What good would middle management do? The answer to that question was a veritable epiphany to me, when I found my physical organization was becoming smaller than the virtual one I was in charge of. A manager must absolutely take stock of whether he is still relevant, of where his impact is. If you head a staff of 100, then no one will wonder about that, but if you manage a virtual department, then things change immensely. Professionals are quickly inclined to think: 'Fine, so that's what you want, but I wonder if that is compatible with my own calendar and targets?' If the compatibility is there, then at least you will have caught their attention. If, however, it is missing, then there is trouble ahead for you, because you no longer control their salary, they have become self-directed and decide on their pay between themselves. In other words, those very professionals are no longer physically in your department and may well start to wonder what your value added is to them."*

Before he was able to find his own answer to this question, Blokhuis had some sleepless nights over this. The first thing to happen was that he realized it was not about himself, but about the employees. At the same time, he was an engineer when he first started work, so he knew: *"After I discovered that other people were actually more adept at engineering, I was able to abandon that chunk of my ego and focus on how to help others realize their own potential. When I made that shift, I began enjoying my new role. It becomes great fun to sit down for a chat with people and, together, examine how they could improve further,"* Blokhuis continues.

In my book *Iedereen CEO* (Everybody CEO), I described how Cisco was setting its eye on virtual collaboration. The CEO at the time, John Chambers, referred to it as the transformation from 'command and control' to 'command and collaborate', a structure for the organization where staffers do not necessarily meet up in departments, be it online or offline, but according to topics and areas of interest, in so-called 'councils'.[29] I question Blokhuis on how this strategy has panned out. He tells me the process moved in a manner similar to a pendulum swinging back and forth. Initially there was a lot of control, then a lot of self-direction and virtual tuning into each other, which proved to actually produce rather too much patchiness and static, and ultimately a swing back to slightly more control. *"You should not flatten an organization too much. People do need leadership. Diversity and virtual collaboration do not become strengths, until they are built on a foundation of conformity and uniformity. A manager is the one to decide what is important. Everyone is allowed to offer their opinions, but the person who is ultimately responsible needs to take decisions. When the pool of people with whom you can collaborate grows exponentially, due to the fact that you are able to transcend physical boundaries, that may be of course interesting but extremely complicated at the same time. A staggering number of cultural aspects pop up. If you meet up with your co-workers more often online than in person, and they turn out to be better versed in the subject at hand than you are, your focus will shift towards encouraging creativity and innovation, in connection with the result, which then translates into maximizing the potential and qualities of the people you work with."*

Using technology to allow professionals, and professionals with leaders, to be attuned to one another will produce an entirely new dynamic which could make or break relationships. We are moving away from a world with an often limited number of relationships, to a world where we are capable of simultaneously maintaining numerous relationships, which will lift us to a whole new level of knowledge transfer and collaboration. Of course, a leader will still maintain their focus on the traditional sides of management, including inciting revenue, optimizing costs, encouraging innovation, devising the strategy and handling conflict within the company. What sets him apart from traditional leaders is that in order to achieve those goals, he will embrace a culture of collaboration which transcends by far anything that traditional structures and management concepts were ever able to.

The countless conversations I have had on the subject, paired with my own experiences, have made clear to me that real-time communication is essential and that this will be of fundamental importance for the credibility and credits any leader can achieve in this day and age. Very often, digital channels can provide an extremely useful instrument for communicating quickly and in an open, transparent and immediate fashion. Today's professionals expect leaders to communicate in real time and in a way that inspires them. They refuse to wait for answers or become entangled in any kind of bureaucracy, in order to find answers. A leader, then, will need to be visible on all channels; they will need to show their 'face' and let their 'voice' be heard. If they fail to do so, their influence will fade away.

Summary

Finding leaders who are committed to constantly improving the organization and its professionals is the call to action which we are receiving in this networking era. Now is the time for leaders who always reach for more value added, who have inquisitive minds and who embrace new ideas, even the unconventional ones. They perceive themselves to be mere facilitators, not the linking pin of the organization. They are there at the right time, but they allow much of their influence to be felt indirectly. They lead by example, particularly in their use of social media.

Epilogue

My publisher asked me to simply write a ksind of exploration of the future, on what 'the market' and our ideas regarding work and organizations would be like in, say, fifteen to twenty years' time. I did something akin to this in *Everybody CEO*, and enjoyed it too, I might add; but it was not without some hesitation. After all, what could be more difficult than making any sort of firm claim about the future, in a time which is changing faster than we can say the word 'change'? Still, I attempt to do just that in all my books, and this book is no exception. Let me try to outline a direction of sorts.

Though we may well wish things were different, a great many organizations are still structured along factory lines. There could be no more fitting title, than that of Intensive Human Farming (Dutch title Intensieve Menshouderij), coined by fellow author Jaap Peters for one of his books. There is a focus on linear procedures, a separation of labor into departments and positions, the old adage 'knowledge equals power', the implicit message that management was superior to craftsmanship: all of it used to suffice. In a world in which everything is now standard; where people have the technological means to find and share information, and where the number of channels through which they do this is practically infinite, organizations actually require access to new ideas and innovation more than ever. The good news is there is no shortage of those. The bad news is that staffers – and clients and other stakeholders alike – are not provided with sufficient facilities to give or contribute to the maximum. Never mind all the flowery speeches, training programs and visionary posters in the staff canteen; all too frequently and far too much, the focus is still on laying down the decisions and checking they are executed.

In the future, success will have a radically different starting point: leaders shall no longer be expected to hold all the answers. In fact, the only way to get ahead in an organization is to tap into the shared knowledge of all the staff members combined. There is no way around digital and social tools. If leaders do not embrace these of their own accord, the tools will force them to. Successful leaders have a strong online presence, similar to what they have in the real world. They do not hide behind a PR department or customer services. Instead, they are there in the front line, having a say on any issue which affects their products and services.

The traditional leader is becoming irrelevant. Nowadays, leaders come to leadership by being respected in the community. They gain this respect when they succeed in fusing individual ideas into one, and empower everyone in the process.

Many leaders find the times to be uncertain. After all, professionals themselves are making a bid for individual leadership, too. Principles which were formerly common are disappearing as we speak. This is especially true for leaders who have been around for some time, have always used a particular working method, and are finding this is becoming less effective. Forced into reinventing themselves, they must return to the very source and ask themselves: 'Remind me, why am I doing this job?' and 'What am I good at?'

Professionals, too, need to face the fact that things have changed irreversibly. They, too, must find out what their value added is. One job for life is soon to be a thing of the past. More often than not, we have serial careers, not in the least because of having to work longer before retirement. It is becoming increasingly important to continue improving yourself within your chosen field, and to join up with other people. The half-life of knowledge (i.e. the time it takes for half of the knowledge on any subject to lose its relevance) keeps shrinking, due to the immense growth in the information which is available. Many fields of expertise can now measure this in months rather than years. Besides, both manual labor and knowledge work are currently being automated at breakneck speed.

Be they salaried workers or self-employed staff in the so-called flexible skin, successful professionals are incomparable in their ability to name their key competences, and to keep them up to date, to boot. They make sensible use of digital technology, tools are used as and when needed;, and in the process they do not make much of a distinction between work and personal life. Because they have up-to-date knowledge and are actively curating and sharing this, they will always stand out under the spotlight of organizations looking for talented people.

Organizations are in effect empty shells. They start 'to breathe' courtesy of the people working there. An awareness on the part of professionals of the need to keep learning, the assumption of responsibility for the organization by those same professionals, paired with achieving the right culture will provide a platform for innovation – for staff, clients and other stakeholders alike; not merely to become more creative, but more loyal too, and for a lower price than ever.

Speedboats, small start-ups founded by young and enterprising professionals, are generally not hampered by any residues from the industrial age. They are flexible organizations, ready to adapt to the world in constant flux. However, they do often find themselves lacking experience and financial room to maneuver. This is precisely why they would often do well to seek out oil tankers to collaborate with. In turn, the oil tankers have a lot to learn from the agile speedboats. Truly savvy oil tankers take the dynamism provided by rotating professionals and use it as an 'extra fast engine'. At times, the flexible skin can temporarily provide some much-needed extra accelerating power.

The main theme in this book is 'adaptability': the ability to transcend what you have learnt in your degree or the things you may even have built your career upon; things like the business models you used to believe in, how relevant you believed your organization to be and how you thought it would remain that way for decades to come. What matters is whether you can accept the transition from the industrial age to the era of networking. Now, more than ever, our collective knowledge is being called to duty. It is the only real way to stay on top of the complexity in our day and age. My wish for you is that you may have smooth sailing!

Menno Lanting
Fall 2015

Notes

Introduction

1   http://www.nbcphiladelphia.com/news/green/So-lar-Trash-Cans-Save-Philadelphia-Millions-200626771.html

2   http://cityclimateleadershipawards.com/barcelona-barcelo-na-smart-city/

3   *Het Financieele Dagblad*, 3 March 2014

4   http://www.irishtimes.com/business/sectors/technolo-gy/smart-sensors-wireless-links-to-make-cities-more-effi-cient-1.1702222

5   http://investorplace.com/2011/05/mcdonalds-nyse-mcd-touch-screen-menu-ordering/#.Ur1fjLTK9oI

6   http://www.google.com/landing/now/

7   http://www.digitaltrends.com/web/everything-you-need-to-know-about-latent-search/

8   *The Everything Store*, Brad Stone

9   Global Institute, 2013

10 'A non-stop stream of data is produced, when you connect a car to the Internet. This data can help you save money, pre-vent the car from breaking down or allow breakdowns to be fixed more quickly,' the ANWB states. http://www.nu.nl/gadgets/3707506/anwb-laat-leden-internetauto-testen.html and http://www.anwb.nl/auto/nieuws/2014/februari/anwb-start-proef-met-connected-car?ovaherk=news-and-tips

11 http://techcrunch.com/2014/01/19/uber-and-disruption/

12 http://www.nu.nl/internet/3788647/uber-wil-taxichauf-

feurs-vervangen-zelfrijdende-autos.html

13 *Big Bang Disruption*, Downes & Nunes, 2014

14 http://www.fastcompany.com/section/most-innovative-com-panies-2014

15 http://www.bcg.com/documents/file42620.pdf

16 http://www.washingtonpost.com/national/on-innovations/digital-darwinism-and-why-brands-die/2011/11/20/gIQAR-2jqlN_story.html

17 *Het Financieele Dagblad*, 4 June 2013

18 http://www.nu.nl/economie/3786775/outlet-was-laatste-stro-halm-frs.html

19 http://www.retailnews.nl/rubrieken/research/research/38755/detailhandel-krimpt-verder-in-2014.html

20 *Het Financieele Dagblad*, 'Adviessectorworsteltnogsteedsmet-moeilijkemarkt',J.PiersmaenP.Kakebeeke,13 September 2013

21 *sioo. De vijf gamechangers voor consulting*, 2013

22 http://www-935.ibm.com/services/us/en/c-suite/csuites-tudy2013/

23 http://www.gallup.com/services/169328/q12-employee-en-gagement.aspx

24 http://www.futuretech.ox.ac.uk/sites/futuretech.ox.ac.uk/files/The_Future_of_Employment_OMS_Working_Paper_1.pdf

25 http://news.nationalgeographic.com/news/2013/07/130719-robot-lfd-pr2-artificial-intelli-gence-crowdsourcing-robotics-machine-learning/

26 *Elsevier Magazine*, 7 June 2014

27 http://www.salon.com/2013/05/12/jaron_lanier_the_inter-net_destroyed_the_middle_class/

28 http://www.mckinsey.com/insights/strategy/the_new_nor-mal

Chapter 1

1 http://www.bostonglobe.com/metro/2014/05/22/taxi-driv-ers-protest-uber-boston-offices/oYlRNohHAHVhcxFIQ2X5aI/story.html, http://techcrunch.com/2014/01/13/an-uber-car-was-attacked-near-paris-as-taxi-drivers-protest-against-ur-

ban-transportation-startups/, http://www.huffingtonpost.
com/2013/06/25/los-angeles-taxi-cab-drivers-protest-
_n_3499229.html and http://skift.com/2014/05/10/london-
taxi-drivers-plan-massive-uber-protest-next-month/

2   http://www.forbes.com/sites/larrydownes/2013/02/06/
lessons-from-uber-why-innovation-and-regulation-dont-
mix/ and http://tech.eu/news/uber-drives-legal-obsta-
cles-time-barcelona/

3   *Harvard Business Review*, March 2013

4   *A dynamic model of process and product innovation*, James M.
Utterback

5   *Success in Changing Environments: Strategies and Key Influencing Factors*, Prof. Dr. Utz Schäffer en Manuela Stol

6   *Fast Second: How Smart Companies Bypass Radical Innovation
to Enter and Dominate New Markets*, Paul Geroski en Constan-
tinos Markides, 2005

7   http://www.newyorker.com/online/blogs/currency/2013/09/
where-nokia-went-wrong.html

8   http://www.engadget.com/2011/02/08/nokia-ceo-stephen-el-
op-rallies-troops-in-brutally-honest-burnin/

9   http://thenextweb.com/asia/2013/10/15/chinas-xiaomi-sells-
100000-of-its-newest-phone-in-86-seconds-and-3000-smart-
tvs-in-2-minutes/

10   http://www.wired.co.uk/promotions/shell-lets-go/innova-
tion/the-idea-factory

11   *Democratizing Innovation*, Eric von Hippel, 2006

12   http://www.mckinsey.com/insights/innovation/hal_varian_
on_how_the_web_challenges_managers

13   *Big bang disruption*, Larry Downes en Paul F. Nunes

14   http://chiefmartec.com/2013/06/martecs-law-technolo-
gy-changes-exponentially-organizations-change-logarithmi-
cally/

15   http://www.mckinsey.com/insights/strategy/leading_in_
the_21st_century_an_interview_with_hertz_ceo_mark_fris-
sora

16   http://www.scribd.com/fullscreen/224608514?access_
key=key-TiQrYKIlOq2iHdtIubdB&allow_share=true&es-

193

cape=false&view_mode=scroll

17 http://diginomica.com/2014/01/23/digital-da-vos-tech-ceos-oust-economists/
18 http://googleblog.blogspot.nl/2010/10/what-were-driving-at.html, http://www.google.com/glass/start/, http://www.google.com/loon/, http://www.americanbanker.com/bank think/google-presents-biggest-threat-to-banking-1059295-1.html
19 http://www.thinkwithgoogle.com/articles/passion-not-perks.html
20 http://m.theglobeandmail.com/report-on-business/careers/career-advice/life-at-work/teluss-collaboration-sherpa-points-the-way-forward/article4491978/?service=mobile
21 *Fortune Magazine*, November 1998
22 http://www.theguardian.com/sustainable-business/access-over-ownership-future-consumption
23 http://www.mckinsey.com/insights/strategy/leading_in_the_21st_century_an_interview_with_hertz_ceo_mark_frissora
24 http://www.nl.capgemini-consulting.com/shopping-2020-delivery
25 World Wide Developers Conference, May 1997
26 *The Everything Store*, Brad Stone
27 http://pazoulay.scripts.mit.edu/docs/hhmi.pdf
28 http://diginomica.com/2014/01/23/digital-da-vos-tech-ceos-oust-economists/
29 http://www.wired.com/2013/08/remembering-the-apple-newtons-prophetic-failure-and-lasting-ideals/
30 http://edge.org/conversation/the-technium
31 http://www.nu.nl/tech/3692932/satya-nadella-nieuwe-ceo-microsoft.html
32 http://www.scribd.com/fullscreen/224608514?access_key=key-TiQrYKIlOq2iHdtIubdB&allow_share=true&escape=false&view_mode=scroll
33 *Telelens op de toekomst*, KPMG 2013
34 http://www.hrmagazine.co.uk/hro/news/1075282/workers-organisations-slow-inflexible-hay-group-research?WT.rss_f=Home&WT.rss_a=Workers+think+or-

ganisations+are+too+slow+and+inflexible,+accord-
ing+to+Hay+Group+research
35 http://www.nexticon.nl/sites/default/files/Innovation_Kill-
ers_How_Financial_Tools_Dest.pdf en *The innovator's dilem-
ma*, Clayton M. Christensen
36 Willem de Bruin, *Historisch Nieuwsblad* nr. 10/2011

Chapter 2

1 http://iveybusinessjournal.com/topics/leadership/distrib-
uted-leadership-at-google-lessons-from-the-billion-dol-
lar-brand#.Uy__W1evC3I
2 *The Rise of the Naked Economy: How to Benefit from the
Changing Workplace*, Ryan Coonerty en Jeremy Neuner
3 http://www.penoactueel.nl/Personeel/Algemeen/2014/6/88-
van-de-managers-wil-personeel-vervangen-1542177W/
4 'Hire by Auditions, Not Resumes', Matt Mullenweg, *Harvard
Business Review*, January 2014
5 http://dupress.com/articles/success-or-struggle-roa-as-
a-true-measure-of-business-performance/?id=us:el:d-
c:dup505:awa:tmt
6 http://www.mt.nl/332/86790/business/ricardo-semler-het-tij-
dperk-van-wijsheid-is-begonnen.html
7 http://www.computable.nl/artikel/nieuws/loop-
baan/4936603/1458016/automatisering-kost-mogeli-
jk-50000-banen.html#ixzz2pEp9aILi
8 *Het Financieele Dagblad*, Friday 5 September 2014
9 http://www.forbes.com/sites/derosetichy/2013/04/15/what-
happens-when-a-hippo-runs-your-company/
10 http://hbr.org/2012/05/the-rise-of-the-supertemp/
11 http://www.youtube.com/watch?v=vyfPZLb3kqc
12 *Harvard Business Review*, December 2013
13 http://webwereld.nl/hardware/80800-vergeet-google-glass--
daar-komt-google-lens
14 http://www.nuzakelijk.nl/zzp/3656214/aandeel-neder-
landse-flexwerkers-verdubbelt.html
15 http://www.nuzakelijk.nl/zzp/3668516/meer-zzpers-
schaarste.html

16 http://www.nuzakelijk.nl/ondernemen/3811324/flexi-
    bele-schil-bedrijven-moet-veel-groter.html
17 http://www.huffingtonpost.com/2013/02/11/philip-park-
    er-books_n_2648820.html
18 http://www.nu.nl/internet/3828135/kunstmatige-intelligen-
    tie-grootste-wikipedia-auteur.html
19 http://rossdawsonblog.com/weblog/archives/2013/06/the-fu-
    ture-of-creativity-and-innovation.html
20 http://www.youtube.com/watch?v=jUo6Lc3EgEs
21 http://www.gallup.com/poll/165269/worldwide-employ-
    ees-engaged-work.aspx
22 http://www.nytimes.com/2012/09/22/business/to-stay-rel-
    evant-in-a-career-workers-train-nonstop.html?pagewant-
    ed=all&_r=0
23 http://news.yahoo.com/marissa-mayer-spent-200-million-hir-
    ing-her-mobile-133939050.html
24 http://www.inc.com/laura-montini/how-to-assemble-your-
    own-personal-board-of-directors.html
25 http://www.gartner.com/newsroom/id/2636073
26 http://www.caop.nl/fileadmin/Bestanden/documenten/cao-
    vanNu/Werken_in_en_aan_verandering.pdf
27 http://www.knooppuntinnovatie.nl/documenten/Volber-
    da%20en%20Van%20Den%20Bosch,%20rethinking%20
    the%20Dutch%20Innovation%20a.pdf
28 'Teaming', *Harvard Business Review*, April 2012
29 http://www.kennisbanksocialeinnovatie.nl/fileupload/NCSI_
    Argumentenkaart_Sociale_Innovatie_-_definitief.pdf
30 *New Rules of Engagement: Life-Work Balance and Employee
    Commitment*, Mike Johnson, 2004
31 *Slim managen & innovatief organiseren*, Henk W. Volberda,
    Frans A.J. van den Bosch en Justin J.P. Jansen, en *Monitor-
    en van sociale innovatie: slimmer werken, dynamisch managen
    en flexibel organiseren*, Henk Volberda, Justin Jansen, Michiel
    Tempelaar en Kevin Heij

Chapter 3

1 http://crowdflower.com/docs/CF-Unilever-CS.pdf
2 http://tinywork.wordpress.com/2013/07/29/crowdflower/

3   *The Discipline of Market Leaders*, Michael Treacy en Fred Wiersema

4   *A Perfect Mess*, Eric Abrahamson en David Freedman

5   *Het Financieele Dagblad*, 1 February 2014

6   http://www.businessweek.com/articles/2014-02-19/facebook-acquires-whatsapp-for-19-billion

7   http://dewerelddraaitdoor.vara.nl/Alexander-Kloepping.3006.0.html

8   http://www.nu.nl/internet/3696037/providers-hadden-met-eigen-whatsapp-dienst-moeten-komen.html

9   http://www.lithium.com/pdfs/casestudies/Lithium-giffgaff-Case-Study.pdf

10 *The Everything Store*, Brad Stone

11 http://money.cnn.com/magazines/fortune/fortune_archive/2003/05/26/343082/

12 http://www.lockheedmartin.com/us/suppliers/supplier-diversity-k.html

13 http://www.prnewswire.com/news-releases/lockheed-martin-strengthens-ties-with-small-diverse-suppliers-through-new-channel-193897171.html

14 http://www.economist.com/news/business/21595435-worlds-biggest-retailer-stumbling-its-genial-new-boss-needs-prove-he-can-push-through

15 http://www.thestreet.com/story/12697841/1/walmart-wmt-surpasses-amazon-amzn-in-online-sales-growth.html

16 http://www.economist.com/news/leaders/21573981-chinas-e-commerce-giant-could-generate-enormous-wealthprovided-countrys-rulers-leave-it

17 http://waset.org/publications/15135/Chinese-Entrepreneurship-in-the-Internet-Age:Lessons-from-Alibaba.com

18 http://waset.org/publications/15135/Chinese-Entrepreneurship-in-the-Internet-Age:Lessons-from-Alibaba.com

19 *The Everything Store*, Brad Stone

20 http://online.wsj.com/news/articles/SB10001424127887324653004578650390383666794

21 http://www.washingtonpost.com/national/jeff-bezos-on-post-purchase/2013/08/05/e5b293de-fe0d-11e2-9711-

370831of6f4d_story.html

22 http://theplazz.com/tweet/fmanjoo_364587833916276740/

23 http://www.nu.nl/beurs/3695508/miljoenenverlies-uitgever-sanoma.html

24 http://www.kpmg.com/NL/nl/IssuesAndInsights/Articles-Publications/Documents/PDF/Innovatie/NewHorizons1.pdf

25 http://johnrichardmartin.com/2013/06/23/sexiest-job-at-sanoma-data-scientist/

26 http://bits.blogs.nytimes.com/2013/11/22/corporate-incubators-popping-up-in-europe/?_php=true&_type=blogs&_r=0

27 http://news.cnet.com/8301-1035_3-57602034-94/samsung-opens-doors-to-new-york-accelerator/

28 https://www.facebook.com/NetherlandsEmbassy/photos

Chapter 4

1 http://www.fastcompany.com/1547686/most-innovative-companies-media

2 http://content.time.com/time/specials/packages/article/0,28804,1879276_1879279_1879212,00.html

3 http://www.theguardian.com/technology/2008/mar/09/blogs

4 http://www.businessinsider.com/seven-secrets-that-led-to-huffington-posts-315000000-success-2011-2

5 http://www.scribd.com/doc/224332847/NYT-Innovation-Report-2014

6 Ibid.

7 http://www.poynter.org/latest-news/top-stories/234303/in-2014-huffpost-live-will-try-to-turn-cool-ideas-into-a-sustainable-business/

8 http://www.hrmagazine.be/nl/newsitem/company-social-media-minder-populair

Chapter 5

1 http://www.nu.nl/beurs/3640703/philips-zet-in-digitalisering-zorg.html

2 Elsevier, 21-28 December 2013

3 https://www.linkedin.com/today/post/article/20140121125357-35894743-there-are-only-two-kinds-of-

companies-which-one-is-yours

4 http://hbr.org/2013/11/you-cant-be-a-wimp-make-the-tough-calls/ar/1

5 http://www.15inno.com/2011/03/27/innovation-lessons-from-02/

6 Read more about this programme in *Versnellen!*, John Kotter, October 2014

7 *Slim managen & innovatief organiseren*, Henk W. Volberda, Frans A. J. van den Bosch, Justin J.P. Jansen

8 *Elsevier*, 19 December 2013

9 http://www.mckinsey.com/insights/business_technology/from_internal_service_provider_to_strategic_partner_an_interview_with_the_head_of_global_business_services_at_p_and_g

10 http://dupress.com/articles/success-or-struggle-roa-as-a-true-measure-of-business-performance/?id=us:el:dc:dup505:awa:tmt

11 http://sloanreview.mit.edu/reports/shifting-social-business/

12 http://sloanreview.mit.edu/article/the-era-of-open-innovation/

Chapter 6

1 http://www.bbc.com/news/technology-25880738

2 http://www.fastcompany.com/3020699/bottom-line/why-intuit-founder-scott-cook-wants-you-to-stop-listening-to-your-boss

3 *Steve Jobs, the Journey is the Reward*, Jeffrey S. Young, 1988

4 *Het Financieele Dagblad*, 1 February 2014

5 http://www.mckinsey.com/insights/strategy/leading_in_the_21st_century_an_interview_with_hertz_ceo_mark_frissora

6 http://www.nytimes.com/2012/02/26/opinion/sunday/innovation-and-the-bell-labs-miracle.html?pagewanted=all&_r=0

7 *The Idea Factory*, Jon Gertner

8 *Harvard Business review*, January/February 2014

9 TNO-rapport *HRM en innovatief werkgedrag: een verkenning*, 2008

10   *The Everything Store,* Brad Stone

11   http://250words.com/2014/01/the-communication-paradox-why-the-best-communication-is-unspoken/#sthash.2E4fCFLv.dpuf

12   http://money.cnn.com/magazines/fortune/fortune_archive/2003/05/26/343082/

13   http://chronicle.com/article/Dont-Confuse-Technology-With/133551/

14   http://www.hrsquare.be/nl/nieuws/5927/35-van-hrmers-zit-niet-op-linkedin

15   http://www.jarche.com/2013/06/social-learning-is-for-human-work/

16   http://www.nytimes.com/2012/04/08/business/phil-libin-of-evernote-on-its-unusual-corporate-culture.html?pagewanted=all&_r=0

17   http://www.wired.com/2013/10/this-hospital-was-designed-to-be-an-innovation-hub/

18   http://www.worldblu.com/awardee-profiles/2013.php

19   http://www.management.wharton.upenn.edu/cappelli/documents/Cappelli_HBR.pdf

20   http://go.quantumworkplace.com/blog/bid/53602/Leadership-360s-are-Best-When-Brought-into-the-Light

21   *Harvard Business review,* January/February 2014

22   http://www.thinkwithgoogle.com/articles/passion-not-perks.html

23   http://www.ted.com/talks/steven_johnson_where_good_ideas_come_from

24   *Enlightenment: Britain and the Creation of the Modern World,* Roy Porter

25   http://www.nytimes.com/2012/02/26/opinion/sunday/innovation-and-the-bell-labs-miracle.html?pagewanted=all&_r=0

26   *BusinessWeek,* 12 October 2004

27   *Brick by Brick: How LEGO Rewrote the Rules of Innovation and Conquered the Global Toy Industry,* David Robertson

28   Ibid.

29   http://hms.harvard.edu/news/close-proximity-leads-better-science-12-15-10

30 http://arxiv.org/ftp/arxiv/papers/1110/1110.2980.pdf
31 *Brick by Brick: How LEG oRewrote the Rules of Innovation and Conquered the Global Toy Industry*, David Robertson
32 http://officesnapshots.com/2012/07/16/pixar-headquarters-and-the-legacy-of-steve-jobs/
33 http://www.fastcompany.com/3003118/zappos-ceo-tony-hsieh-focusing-collisions
34 http://www.carlsonschool.umn.edu/assets/71190.pdf
35 http://www.inc.com/ilan-mochari/creativity-messy-offices.html
36 http://www.hrsquare.be/nl/nieuws/5927/35-van-hrmers-zit-niet-op-linkedin
37 *Managementboek magazine*, May 2013
38 http://papers.ssrn.com/sol3/papers.cfm?abstract_id=1709943
39 *Harvard Business Review*, December 2013
40 https://search.cern.ch/Pages/default.aspx
41 http://www.unesco.org/new/en/media-services/single-view/news/cern_and_unesco_60_years_of_science_for_peace/back/9597/#.U8OQVrHmeDk
42 http://www.quantumworkplace.com/leadership-360s-are-best-when-brought-into-the-light/
43 *Culture Shock: A Handbook For 21st Century Business*, Will McInnes
44 http://www.worldblu.com/awardee-profiles/2013.php
45 http://thecollaborationimperative.com/2012/11/why-collaboration-matters/
46 *Harper's Magazine*, September 1932, 'Edison in His Laboratory;, Martin André Rosanoff
47 http://www.google.com/about/company/facts/culture/
48 http://www.thinkwithgoogle.com/articles/passion-not-perks.html
49 https://www.randstad.nl/over-randstad/pers/persberichten/2014/03/werkmonitor-kwart-heeft-niet-genoeg-energie-om-elke-dag-te-werken
50 http://herald-review.com/business/national-and-international/employers-push-workers-to-disconnect/article_8dc1b-f6a-60c8-11e3-a630-001a4bcf887a.html

51 http://en.wikipedia.org/wiki/Kranzberg%27s_laws_of_technology

52 http://archive.wired.com/wired/archive/8.04/joy_pr.html

53 *Harvard Business Review*, September 2011

54 http://www.wired.co.uk/magazine/archive/2013/12/features/hyperstimulation/viewgallery/330469

55 *Reading Strategies for Coping With Information Overload ca. 1550-1700*, Ann Blair

56 *Too Big to Know: Rethinking Knowledge Now That the Facts Aren't the Facts, Experts Are Everywhere, and the Smartest*, David Weinberger

57 http://theamericanscholar.org/solitude-and-leadership/#.UyFr2YWvC3I

58 http://www.realtimeperformance.com/RealTimeLeadership/?p=770

59 http://www.theatlantic.com/magazine/archive/2008/07/is-google-making-us-stupid/306868

60 http://nl.wikipedia.org/wiki/Serendipiteit

61 http://www.ethanzuckerman.com/blog/2008/06/09/the-architecture-of-serendipity

62 *Harvard Business Review*, January/February 2014

63 http://www.businessinsider.com/management-tip-of-the-day-reed-hastings-2010-6#ixzz31aiDAXbZ

64 TNO-rapport *HRM en innovatief werkgedrag: een verkenning,* 2008

65 *Harvard Business Review*, January/February 2014

66 http://tech.fortune.cnn.com/2011/08/25/how-apple-works-inside-the-worlds-biggest-startup/

67 *Steve Jobs*, Walter Isaacson

68 *Brick by Brick: How LEGO Rewrote the Rules of Innovation and Conquered the Global Toy Industry*, David Robertson

Chapter 7

1 http://www.fastcompany.com/3001275/experimentation-new-planning

2 http://blogs.valvesoftware.com/abrash/valve-how-i-got-here-

what-its-like-and-what-im-doing-2/

3   http://www.valvesoftware.com/company/Valve_Handbook_
    LowRes.pdf

4   Ibid.

5   http://www.slideshare.net/zaugnakhaldun/valve-employ-
    ee-handbook

6   http://www.fastcompany.com/1801532/ign-employees-use-vi-
    ral-pay-system-determine-each-others-bonuses

7   http://www.zapposinsights.com/blog/item/6-ways-to-build-
    employee-engagement-and-relationships-in-your-company

8   http://www.businessweek.com/articles/2012-04-12/how-to-
    set-your-employees-free-reed-hastings

9   *The Connected Company*, Dave Gray

10 http://www.dol.gov/odep/topics/youth/softskills/softskills.
    pdf

11 http://www.forbes.com/sites/forbesleadershipfo-
    rum/2012/05/14/how-my-company-made-truly-open-manage-
    ment-work/

12 https://www.youtube.com/watch?v=SoeNXQq85-4

13 http://www.worldblu.com/awardee-profiles/2013.php

14 Ibid.

15 'Verdraaide organisaties', Wouter Hart, *Managementboek
    Magazine*, January 2014

16 http://www.slideshare.net/reed2001/culture-1798664

17 http://vineetnayar.delos.za.net/leadership-and-business-les-
    sons/destroying-the-office-of-the-ceo/

Chapter 8

1   http://www.kenblanchard.com/img/pub/pdf_critical_leader-
    ship_skills.pdf

2   *Cases in Leadership*, W. Glenn Rowe en Laura Guerrero

3   http://www.nrc.nl/carriere/2013/04/02/wij-mensen-zijn-van-
    nature-volgers/

4   http://www.managers.org.uk/news/half-workers-quit-jobs-
    due-bad-management

5   Oosterhout, 2 June 2011

6   http://leaderlab.com/why-join/

7   'The Path to Glory Is Paved With Hierarchy: When Hierarchical Differentiation Increases Group Effectiveness', *Psychological Science*, June 2012

8   http://forbesindia.com/printcontent/33893

9   *Maverick!*, Ricardo Semler

10 Ibid.

11 http://content.spencerstuart.com/sswebsite/pdf/lib/Talent3-0.pdf

12 http://hbr.org/2009/12/to-be-a-better-leader-give-up-authority/ar/1

13 http://www.businessinsider.com/radical-transparency-in-small-business-2013-1

14 http://www.valvesoftware.com/company/people.html

15 TNO-rapport *HRM en innovatief werkgedrag: een verkenning*, 2008

16 *De flexibele onderneming: strategieën voor succesvol concurreren*, Henk Volberda

17 *Harvard Business Review*, November 2013

18 http://www.bbc.com/news/technology-25880738

19 http://mkbkrachtcentrale.nl/slimste-bedrijf-2011/

20 'How leaders can build innovative organizations', *The African Business Review*

21 http://www.mt.nl/513/83124/gezond-ondernemen-verzuim/hoe-kun-je-duurzame-inzetbaarheid-stimuleren.html

22 http://www.fastcompany.com/3003122/khan-academy-founder-sal-khan-not-being-autocrat

23 https://www.yammer.com/pdfs/case_study_deloitte.pdf

24 http://www.marketingmagazine.co.uk/article/1170028/social-brands-lego-forces-management-sit-social-media-exams

25 'Generations in the workplace: Winning the generation game', *The Economist*, September 2013

26 http://online.wsj.com/article/SB10000872396390444083304578018423363962886.html?mod=WSJ_hps_MIDDLENexttoWhatsNewsFifth

27 *Harvard Business Review*, December 2013

28 http://www.kenan-flagler.unc.edu/executive-development/custom-programs/~/media/827B6E285F2141C49D407DF7E-

5F5A1C4.ashx

29 https://www.youtube.com/watch?v=9WX7BNnYTf8

www.ingramcontent.com/pod-product-compliance
Lightning Source LLC
Chambersburg PA
CBHW021557210326
41599CB00010B/491